Also by Marian Burros

The New Elegant but Easy Cookbook (with Lois Levine)

20-Minute Menus

Eating Well Is the Best Revenge

Keep It Simple: 30-Minute Meals from Scratch

The Best of De Gustibus

Pure and Simple

You've Got It Made

The Elegant but Easy Cookbook (with Lois Levine)

Second Helpings (with Lois Levine)

Freeze with Ease (with Lois Levine)

The Summertime Cookbook (with Lois Levine)

Come for Cocktails, Stay for Supper (with Lois Levine)

Marian Burros may be contacted at
her e-mail address: marbur@nytimes.com

SIMON & SCHUSTER   New York London Toronto Sydney Singapore

MARIAN BURROS

COOKING
for COMFORT

More Than 100 Wonderful Recipes That Are as Satisfying to Cook as They Are to Eat

SIMON & SCHUSTER
Rockefeller Center
1230 Avenue of the Americas
New York, NY 10020

SIMON & SCHUSTER and colophon are registered
trademarks of Simon & Schuster, Inc.

For information regarding special discounts for bulk purchases,
please contact Simon & Schuster Special Sales at:
1-800-456-6798 or business@simonandschuster.com

Designed by Bonni Leon-Berman

Manufactured in the United States of America

10   9   8   7   6   5   4   3   2   1

Library of Congress Cataloging-in-Publication Data is available

ISBN 0-7432-3681-5

To my mother, Dorothy, who taught me how to cook

And to my children, Michael and Ann,
who carry on in her tradition in the kitchen ❧

ACKNOWLEDGMENTS

*I*n the middle of testing the lemon meringue pie recipe for this book, I had an epiphany. It dawned on me that, once again, I was working with one of my mother's recipes. Thirty years after my mother died, I had finally realized what an enormous culinary influence she had on me.

I had never stopped to think about it. When I finally had a kitchen of my own, I couldn't wait to experiment with dishes that were different from my mother's—despite the fact that my mother was a very good cook.

Of course, I called her when I wanted to know how to roast a chicken (Ah! First you have to take the package of chicken parts *out* of the chicken's cavity) or make a pot roast (I see: The reason the meat burned on the bottom was because I used a thin aluminum pot), but I also wanted to make Southern fried chicken and lobster fra diavolo, strawberries Romanoff, and pumpkin chiffon pie.

Even before Julia Child arrived on the scene, I was taking classes with Dione Lucas, a Cordon Bleu–trained Englishwoman. She may have been the first television chef, and from her I learned how to bone a chicken and turn it inside out, a skill I have never used since. I also learned how to make her chocolate roll (you'll find it on page 172).

Of course, after Julia I completely Frenchified my kitchen with copper pots and imported knives and dishes for soufflés and gratins, and molds for crème caramel and *mousse au chocolat*. But I still use some of the tools my mother passed on to me and have been eternally sorry I did not keep her potato masher.

It wasn't until I went to work on this book and back to the dishes I have loved best that it came to me: I am my mother's daughter, even in the kitchen. This love of cooking has been passed on to both of my children; it always makes me smile when my daughter, Ann, calls and asks for advice on making a dish. She is an instinctive cook and probably never reads recipes.

My son, Michael, the lawyer, cooks in his restaurant kitchen in Spain. He is the owner and chef of O Cabaliño do Demo, in Santiago de Compostela, in Galicia, the northwest corner of Spain, where he has far surpassed my cooking skills. (Honestly, it's not a mother's pride talking; my son's food at his vegetarian restaurant is superb.)

Along with the recipes that credit my mother—the meat sauce and the brisket, the chicken soup and the mushroom and barley soup, the coffee cake and the lemon meringue pie—you will note a number that come from Michael—chocolate and butterscotch puddings, mocha brownies, and eggplant lasagna, among others. Influence goes both ways.

There are many other people I am eager to thank, most especially Susan Simon, whose professional name is SueChef. As in the past, she not only tested recipes for me that I wanted a second set of taste buds to try, but she contributed a few of her own. And I also thank my son, Michael, for providing some of the best recipes in the book and for testing a few others.

Thanks to Roy Coleman, my significant other, for sampling the experiments, good and bad, and for making the wine suggestions.

To Sam Sifton, editor of the "Dining In, Dining Out" section of *The New York Times*, I am particularly grateful for his deft and graceful editing of the Introduction to the book.

I am indebted to Harold McGee, the author of *On Food and Cooking* (Simon & Schuster, 1997) and scientist extraordinaire, who graciously answered all my chemistry questions.

To Elsa Castro, who has made my life easier in the kitchen for more than twenty years, special thanks.

My agent, Amanda Urban, and my book editor, Sydny Miner, have always been there as sounding boards and to lean on.

But my most special thanks go to my mother, who taught me the importance of family meals and cooking with love—even if it took me decades to realize my debt to her.

Marian Fox Burros
Northeast Kingdom, Vermont
November 2002

CONTENTS

COOKING
for COMFORT

INTRODUCTION

Roughly three years ago, for reasons that now seem as unfathomable and obvious as a shift in the weather, I began to long for the simple, straightforward food of my childhood. After spending close to two decades putting together recipes for quick-cooking dinners appropriate to a fast-paced urban lifestyle—food that could be put on a table 20 minutes after coming home from work—I just wanted to take the kind of time my mother could afford to put a meal on the table. I wanted the food my mother made for me.

This return to simple pleasures has been under way in America's restaurant kitchens for a couple of years. It is part of an evolutionary process. Now that American chefs know they can cook as well as anyone in the world, they don't have to prove it anymore. As consumers, we've gone from coveting food from abroad to coveting food from the local farmer. Today, in the culinary world, the phrase "locally grown" has as high a standing on menus as fancy ingredients like foie gras and truffles. We want artisanal food, not corporate ingredients. We want meat that is organic and grass-fed, not stockyard-raised or bioengineered.

In fact, in some ways we have come to a point where the quality of the ingredients is more important than any fussing done with them. These two directions—on the one hand a desire to return to the satisfying, family-based meals of America's past; and on the other hand the desire to eat healthy, family-farm-based ingredients—have led to the reappearance of what has commonly come to be called comfort food. We are embracing dishes particular to America, reinterpreting them in some instances, leaving them as they stand in others. This process is part of a natural cycle, too. Many of us have become bored with the refinements that some chefs had been visiting on their dishes, just to one-up their colleagues, it seemed. Eating out at some restaurants required too much work.

Not coincidentally, this change in viewpoint has also led to the publication of this book—which brings me back to my mother again. When she started cooking, most of what was available fresh was regional. Not much was being shipped across the country, and almost nothing came from abroad. That meant we ate corn in the summer, and it meant that she bought it at the farm on which it was grown, about 15 minutes away from our house in Waterbury, Connecticut. The farmer sold corn that he picked twice a day, nothing else. My mother always went to him late in the afternoon, after the final picking, so that the corn was just out of the field and half an hour later was in the pot. And she examined every ear, pulling back the husk a little to see if there were worms. (Pesticides had not yet arrived on the scene.) Today, if I see a worm in the corn, I'm thrilled!

My mother's chickens and eggs also came from a nearby farm, though she bought them at a market; we thought a double-yolk egg a happy miracle then. The milk was delivered by a milkman, and it had cream on the top, a big treat for cereal in the morning.

After World War II, though, something happened to our food—the way we grew it, processed it, and shipped it. None of it was good. Only in the last 20 years, in fact, have we started to react to the terrible crimes against taste that were committed on American farms in the name of efficiency, cheap prices, and uniformity. Today, thank goodness, we can find food as good as, and often better than, what my mother had available to her. That makes simple cooking far more rewarding than trying to create restaurant meals at home.

This craving for simplicity and for Mother's cooking crystallized for me on September 11, 2001. Not just for me, it seems, but for other Americans as well. First our desire for comfort food was an effort to assure ourselves that the world had not come to an end, even if the world as we knew it had. Now it is an assurance that everything is still, somehow, all right.

In the days and weeks that followed, in my kitchen, as in others around the country, recipes for meat loaf, tapioca pudding, lemon meringue pie, toasted cheese sandwiches, and tomato soup were retrieved from the dusty recesses of kitchen cabinets.

A month after the attack I wrote a column for *The New York Times* about this rush to pamper ourselves at the table. Recounting a story told to me by Joan Hamburg, the WOR radio talk-show host in New York City, I wrote: "Even the X-ray thin have thrown caution to the winds, in search of the familiar, the comfortable."

Joan had been clucking over the behavior of guests at lunch during a football game. "All those thin women dove into the chicken potpie and the corn bread and the double chocolate mousse pie," she said. "That potpie with its wicked crust—you can't believe how they were mopping up the sauce from it with bread."

The article struck a chord with readers, one my editor at Simon & Schuster, Sydny Miner, heard right away. "It's the stuff that makes me feel safe," she said. *Cooking for Comfort* was born.

When life gets more uncertain, more stressful than usual, we look to foods that made us feel secure as children. For those of us who were brought up on the twentieth-century American diet, that means meat loaf dressed with catsup, buttery mashed potatoes, and chocolate chip cookies.

I went rummaging through my recipe box, which had been sitting on the top shelf of a cabinet, well out of reach. In it I found the treats of my childhood, many of which I had abandoned in the first flush of my own independence and adulthood. The writing on many of the 3-by-5 cards was in my mother's hand.

But *Cooking for Comfort* couldn't be just about my family's cooking, and so I queried my friends, and sometimes perfect strangers, to come up with a list of recipes about which most people would agree: macaroni and cheese, spaghetti with marinara sauce, brownies, crab cakes, onion soup, cheesecake, and, of course, meat loaf and mashed potatoes, as well as dishes that are not so universally applauded, like tapioca pudding and cheese grits.

There are probably some comfort foods you will look for on the pages of this book that you will not find. My editor said that nothing made her feel more comfortable than the smell of coconut roasting in the oven, because her mother made coconut cake every Christmas. Others told me how much they loved Grape-nuts pudding or tongue sandwiches. But those didn't make the final cut.

No, this book, for all my attempts to broaden its appeal, is a very personal one; it comes from my family heritage and from where I was brought up. As a result, it appears well anchored in an East Coast tradition, though I have striven mightily to include recipes from elsewhere in the country. (A friend from the Northwest said that turkey burgers were a great comfort food out there. I must have had the wrong recipe.)

There are, however, some East Coast classics that I could not in good conscience include. Chicken tetrazzini really is an awful creation. Three tries and it was out. I attempted to resurrect a molded potato salad with which I won a trip to Europe but today cannot imagine why. And what ever did I see in my recipe for pumpkin chiffon pie? On the other hand, when the twentieth or twenty-third person told me that grilled cheese sandwiches and tomato soup were definitely comforting, I produced a recipe for cream of tomato soup. Campbell's it is not. It's better.

Much of this food is not food anyone would want to eat every day because, by definition, most comfort food is creamy and buttery and often sweet. Still, there are some recipes that fit right into a healthful diet, and I learned as I went along that there are substitutes that can be made to lower a dish's calorie count without destroying its integrity. In the book most of these recipes are described as "streamlined."

Of course, for some people it is not just the act of eating the meat loaf or lemon meringue pie that is soothing; it is the act of cooking them. Taking time to put something together offers concrete proof of effort. Cooking takes a certain amount of concentration; it's hard to think of the complex and sometimes frightening problems of the day over which you have no control when you have to think about something over which you actually can exercise control—what you are doing right now. I had, frankly, forgotten how satisfying and peaceful it is to take my time when cooking. I loved every moment of recipe testing for this book . . .

With one possible exception, that is. Eight tries at popovers and I never got one I liked well enough to include without buying cast-iron muffin pans, even though popovers were once a favorite of mine.

Comfort food is here to stay, it seems. Though the immediate fear and depression that followed 9/11/01 have receded, people are still uneasy because we are living at a time of enormous uncertainty. We are in the midst of a new kind of war, even as we experience the aftereffects of a burst economic bubble and the sometimes illegal activities of the captains of industry who have let us all down.

Meals with family or friends help us forget about that. We want to go back to a time when life was not so complicated—or, at least, when we look at it from a distance, it was one that seemed much simpler. One of the few ways most of us can get there together is through our food.

And, in fact, what we can have on our tables today is a good deal better in some ways than what we could have had in the good old days—there are many more quality ingredients available to us as a nation and greater knowledge within it about cooking. My mother couldn't buy fresh mozzarella or fresh goat cheese. She had only one baking chocolate from which to choose. In the last fifty years we've learned a lot.

There is progress in *Cooking for Comfort*, too.

HOW TO USE THIS BOOK

*S*ome of the recipes in this book, like the Plum Torte, are classics. Some have been tweaked, like the shortcake, because even with simple and old-fashioned recipes there are more sophisticated techniques, and sometimes better ingredients, with which to work. A few dishes have had a major overhaul, like the chicken potpie. The headnotes of each recipe go into some detail about changes.

Because I spent so many years creating good, healthful, low-calorie food, I couldn't resist playing with some of the recipes to create what I have called a "streamlined" version, without disturbing the integrity of the flavor and texture of the finished dish. It's possible to make coleslaw and potato salad with light mayonnaise and no one can tell the difference. Other recipes are just naturally healthful, like Mushroom Barley Soup (page 60) or Linguine with Red Clam Sauce (page 108). But it is not possible to make a low-fat coconut cake, or at least not one that you would want to eat.

You may notice that some recipes call for olive oil; others call for extra virgin olive oil. For cooking I use olive oil, because cooking destroys the delicate flavors of the extra virgin. In salads, or for drizzling on an already cooked dish, extra virgin olive oil is preferred.

Some recipes call for sifted flour. That means to measure *after* sifting. Some call for unsifted flour. That means to measure *before* sifting. Even if the instructions then say to sift again after measuring, there is no need to measure a second time. The delicacy of the finished product determines whether sifting before measuring is necessary.

Roy Coleman, my significant other, selected generic wines that sell for $10 or $15, appropriate, he says, for comfort food.

Some recipes can be prepared ahead and refrigerated and/or frozen. Instructions on how to do that are given with each of those recipes. In a few places I have said reluctantly that a dish, like mashed potatoes, could be made ahead and reheated, but warned that it would not really be as good. Sometimes you have to be practical and compromise.

Most of this cooking is the kind you want to do when you want to cook or when cooking will give you pleasure, not when you need to throw something together in order to eat. For most of us that means cooking on the weekend, or cooking when you have to bring a single dish to a party. This is not food to be rushed. It is food to be savored, both while it is being prepared and when it is eaten.

After working with dozens of brands of key ingredients, I've decided to name names because often the brand *does* make a difference. There are a few commercial foods—mayonnaise and sour cream, in particular—that are head and shoulders above their competitors. You probably figured that out a long time ago, but for those who haven't, they are Hellmann's mayonnaise on the East Coast, Best Foods mayonnaise west of the Rockies, and Breakstone's sour cream in the East, and Knudson's in the West. Hellmann's Light is also excellent if you want to cut out some calories, and Breakstone's low fat is quite good. I also prefer Grand Marnier to other orange liqueurs. Whenever a recipe uses an ingredient that might not be available in smaller cities, I have tried to offer a Web site where it is possible to order it by mail. See Sources, pages 203–4.

COMFORT FOOD FOR
EVERYDAY GOOD HEALTH

Comfort food does not always mean butter and cream and sugar, large quantities of which you may not want to eat every day. Many comfort foods are dishes that would fit into anyone's sensible diet.

The following dishes belong on everyone's healthy eating plan. Some require the change in the variety of mayonnaise or yogurt; others are perfect as is.

BREAKFAST
and BRUNCH

BLUEBERRY PANCAKES

𝓑uttermilk makes a much lighter and more tender pancake than plain milk. With or without the blueberries, these are the pancakes everyone remembers but hardly anyone gets to eat anymore.

yield: 15 pancakes

1½ cups sifted unbleached all-purpose flour
3 tablespoons sugar
1¼ teaspoons baking powder
¼ teaspoon baking soda
¼ teaspoon salt
1½ cups buttermilk

3 tablespoons unsalted melted butter, cooled a little
2 lightly beaten eggs
1 cup fresh blueberries
¼ to ½ teaspoon finely grated lemon rind
Pan spray or oil
Maple syrup and butter for serving

1. Sift together the sifted flour, sugar, baking powder, baking soda, and salt.

2. Gently mix in the buttermilk, butter, and eggs. Do not overmix.

3. Fold in the blueberries and the lemon rind.

4. Over medium-high heat, heat a large nonstick skillet until it is hot. Spray or rub with a little oil.

5. From a large mixing spoon, gently drop the batter into the pan. Do not crowd the pancakes. Reduce the heat to medium. Cook until bubbles begin to form. Flip the pancakes and continue cooking for another couple of minutes. Pancakes should be golden brown. Serve with maple syrup and butter.

VARIATION: *You can substitute raspberries for the blueberries, or make the pancakes without the berries and lemon rind.*

HELP NOTE: *If blueberries are not in season, use frozen berries. Fresh blueberries out of season are often unbelievably sour.*

To make ahead, mix all the dry ingredients together the day before and store in a covered container. Wash and dry the blueberries and set aside. Just before cooking, add the wet ingredients.

Adding lemon zest to the batter perks up the blueberries. Adjust the amount according to sweetness of berries.

Make sure the butter and syrup for topping the pancakes are at room temperature. 🌿

POTATO PANCAKES

*M*y favorite potato pancakes have always been very thin and very crisp. They remind me of potato chips—you can't eat just one.

In a story Joan Nathan did for *The New York Times* about the potato pancakes made by Daniel Boulud of the four-star Restaurant Daniel in New York City, I discovered a chef who likes them the same way. Boulud uses chives in place of the traditional onion, and I have appropriated the idea.

I'd serve these for brunch, breakfast, or supper.

yield: 4 pancakes

2 pounds new potatoes, peeled
3 lightly beaten eggs
6 tablespoons chopped fresh chives

Salt and freshly ground black pepper
  to taste
Olive oil for sautéing

1. Grate the potatoes on the thinnest grater of a food processor. Place the potatoes in a mixing bowl and combine thoroughly with the eggs, chives, salt, and pepper.

2. Over high heat, heat about 1 tablespoon or a little more oil in a medium nonstick sauté pan. Divide the potato mixture in quarters and scoop up one quarter of the mixture in your hands. Squeeze out the liquid.

3. Reduce the heat to medium-low. Place the potato mixture in the middle of the pan and with a spatula and your hands spread it out as thinly as possible to reach the sides of the pan.

4. Cook about 5 minutes, until the bottom browns (you will be able to see the browning).

5. Place a plate the same size as the pan over the pancake and flip the pancake onto the plate, then slide the pancake back into the pan and continue cooking about 4 more minutes to brown the bottom. Flip the pancake out onto a plate. Repeat with the oil and remaining potatoes until all the batter is used.

6. Serve plain or with any of the usual accompaniments.

HELP NOTE: *What did we do before we had nonstick pans? They make cooking like this so easy!*

This is the kind of dish that calls for cooking in the kitchen with guests gathered around.

I confess I can do without the usual accoutrements: These pancakes are sensational without adornment. However, the following garnishes are delicious: thinly sliced strips of smoked salmon; sour cream or a mixture of sour cream and plain nonfat yogurt, using a ratio of 3 to 1; Crème Fraîche (page 167); or even caviar. ❦

REUBEN'S APPLE PANCAKE

$\mathcal{M}$y first encounter with the Reuben's Pancake is recounted in a 1986 column I wrote for *The New York Times*.

A college friend invited me and another girl to join her, her father, and her grandfather for a weekend in Manhattan. "Because of the weather we had to take a train from Boston and arrived too late to eat anywhere but in a restaurant open twenty-four hours a day.

"While I remember a great deal about the restaurant's décor, I remember nothing about the food except the sublimely rich twelve-inch pancake.

"Italian marble, gold-leaf ceiling, lots of walnut paneling, and dark red leather seats—to a small-town girl it was the quintessential New York City restaurant."

I had devised a recipe in 1986 for this once nationally famous 12-inch pancake filled with apples and covered with caramelized sugar (it took five tries, 30 eggs, and 2½ pounds of butter), so you can imagine my surprise upon seeing it in a December 2001 issue of *The New York Times Magazine*. Without credit!

My own newspaper!

I confess, it offered a slight improvement that was not spelled out in my version: how to flip a 12-inch pancake easily. And it took advantage of a nonstick skillet, a piece of equipment that was not available in 1986.

After my recipe appeared in the *Times*, Libby Hillman, a cookbook author and cooking teacher, wrote me a letter: "Before I wrote my first cookbook (in 1963) I was invited into the kitchen to witness the apple pancake from beginning to end.

"Everything you said was absolutely correct, but Arnold Reuben, Jr., forgot one important fact. The caramelization was accomplished by setting the entire pancake in flames. Plenty of butter and sugar produced a great flame and heavy candy coating. Oddly enough I do not remember the raisins."

Restaurants come and go and so do food fads, but that 12-inch pancake has never been topped, not even equaled.

Though it's too rich for breakfast, it is perfect for brunch or for supper, or maybe for a late night if you forgot to eat dinner.

The night I made it again, I ate half of it; there are some who eat the whole thing.

1 large green apple

2 tablespoons raisins, optional (I like them)

1½ tablespoons PLUS about 6 tablespoons sugar

½ teaspoon ground cinnamon

3 eggs

½ cup milk (I used 1 percent because it was what I had in the house; you can use whatever you have)

½ cup unbleached all-purpose flour

⅛ teaspoon pure vanilla extract

8 tablespoons (1 stick) unsalted butter

¼ cup rum

1. Peel, quarter, and core the apple and slice it into ¼-inch-thick quarter-moon-shaped slices. Place in a bowl with raisins, if using, 1½ tablespoons sugar, and the cinnamon. Stir well; cover and marinate for at least an hour but up to a day if you like. Stir occasionally.

2. Whisk the eggs. Mix a little of the milk with the flour to make a paste. Whisk in the rest of the milk. Whisk the eggs into the milk-flour mixture to make a smooth batter and beat in vanilla.

3. In a 12-inch nonstick skillet, heat 2 tablespoons butter until it sizzles. Add the apples and raisins and cook over medium heat, stirring, about 5 minutes, until the apples soften. Add another 2 tablespoons butter and melt. Pour in the batter and cook over medium-high heat, pulling the sides of the pancake away from the edges and allowing the batter to flow under and cook. When the pancake begins to firm up, sprinkle 2 tablespoons of the sugar evenly over the top.

4. Flip the pancake by placing a cookie sheet over the skillet and turning the pancake onto the sheet. Add 2 more tablespoons of butter to the pan; melt it. Slip the pancake back into the pan; allow the bottom to caramelize, about 2 minutes.

5. Sprinkle the top of the pancake with another 2 tablespoon of sugar and repeat the flipping procedure. Melt another 2 tablespoons butter in the skillet and slip the pancake back into the pan and caramelize the bottom, another 2 minutes.

6. Sprinkle with 2 tablespoons sugar and repeat the flipping. Return to the heat. Sprinkle with the rum and flame. When the flames die, serve the pancake.

HELP NOTE: *The recipe originally called for a skillet with sloping sides, but you can do it in a straight-sided skillet, too. Because it is nonstick, any skillet shape will work.*

To get a head start: Marinate the apple mixture overnight; mix together the eggs, milk, flour, and vanilla, as in step 2. Refrigerate. Return to room temperature and continue with step 3 through 7. ❦

BUTTERMILK WAFFLES

I resurrected my 1952 waffle iron to make these. It still does a wonderful job. My son says he doesn't remember my making waffles for him when he was a child. Did I force him to eat frozen toaster oven waffles? I hope not. There is no comparison.

yield: about 3 large waffles

2 cups sifted unbleached all-purpose flour
I teaspoon salt
½ teaspoon baking soda
2 eggs, separated

1¾ cups buttermilk
4 tablespoons (½ stick) melted unsalted
   butter, slightly cooled
Maple syrup and butter for serving

1. Preheat the waffle iron.

2. Sift the flour with the salt and baking soda.

3. Beat the egg yolks and beat in the buttermilk.

4. Add the dry ingredients to the buttermilk mixture and mix only to blend; do not overmix. Stir in the melted butter.

5. Beat the egg whites until stiff but not dry and fold them into the batter; do not blend completely.

6. Following the directions for your waffle iron, bake the waffles until they are crisp and brown on the outside and soft inside. Serve with butter and maple syrup, of course.

HELP NOTE: *To get a quick start in the morning, prepare the dry ingredients the night before, store in a covered container, and set aside.*

Buttermilk produces the most tender waffles, fluffy inside and crisp outside. Experiment with your waffle iron to get just the right degree of crispness outside without drying out the waffles.

I have made waffles with sugar and without; without is just as good as with, and when maple syrup is poured over them, no one could tell the difference.

When buying maple syrup, do not choose the fancy grade. The syrup with the most intense, and I think the best, flavor is Grade B or Amber.

Be sure to have the butter and syrup at room temperature. 🌿

RITZ-CARLTON BLUEBERRY MUFFINS

*W*hen I first ate blueberry muffins at the Ritz-Carlton, there was only one Ritz-Carlton, *the* Ritz-Carlton in Boston. The hotel has been serving some version of them since it opened in 1927. This recipe was created in the 1980s, and I'm sticking with it. The secret is the crusty, sugared topping.

yield: about 12 muffins

3½ cups sifted unbleached all-purpose
    flour
3 tablespoons baking powder
1½ cups sugar
Pinch salt

5 lightly beaten eggs
½ cup milk
8 tablespoons (1 stick) unsalted butter,
    melted and cooled
5 cups blueberries, fresh or frozen

1. Place a rack in the middle of the oven; preheat the oven to 425 degrees.

2. Grease the tops of large muffin tins and insert paper muffin cups in each opening. If using a nonstick muffin pan, greasing and muffin cups are unnecessary.

3. Mix the flour, baking powder, ¾ cup of the sugar, and salt together by hand. Stir in the eggs, milk, and butter; do not overmix. Carefully fold in the berries. (The batter is very thick.)

4. Mound the batter in the muffin tins about ¼ inch from the top of the tin and sprinkle with the remaining sugar.

5. Reduce the heat to 400 degrees and bake the muffins for about 20 minutes. Test by inserting a cake tester in the center. If it comes out clean the muffins are done; otherwise, return the muffins to the oven for a few more minutes.

6. Remove the muffins from the tins and cool a little on a rack. Serve.

HELP NOTE: *For larger muffins, bake in greased custard cups and bake about 5 minutes longer.*

If blueberries are not in season, use frozen berries. Fresh blueberries out of season are often unbelievably sour.

Like all muffins, these do not taste better the second day. The same is true, but to a lesser extent, if the muffins are frozen. But if you want to have these for weekend guests, you can save yourself a little time in the morning by having the dry ingredients mixed together the night before; just store them in a covered container; wash and dry the blueberries. Add the wet ingredients in the morning. ❦

CHEESE OMELET

If I ate whatever I wanted, I would have a cheese omelet every day for breakfast.

Eggs are versatile, but they are also very delicate and must be treated with respect. My preference in omelets is for what the French call *baveuse*—very soft on the inside. Cook it too long and it becomes rubbery. If you are an aficionado of omelets, it's worth it to buy an omelet pan and use it for nothing else. A finely grated Cheddar is perfect because it must melt quickly without a tremendous amount of heat.

Beat two eggs just enough to let a few bubbles form; season with a bit of salt and pepper. Heat the omelet pan with a tablespoon of unsalted butter and, over high heat, pour in the eggs. Let the eggs set for about 10 seconds and then, using a long narrow spatula, keep pulling the eggs away from the sides, tipping the pan so that the uncooked egg can fill in those spaces.

When most of the egg has coagulated, sprinkle on about 2 tablespoons of cheese, fold the omelet in half, and cook for another 30 seconds. Slide out onto a plate and serve. This recipe makes one serving.

SPANISH TORTILLA

This recipe is adapted from chef Xoan at O Cabaliño do Demo, my son's restaurant in Santiago de Compostela, Spain.

The technique for making a traditional tortilla calls for cooking the potatoes in a lot of oil over low heat so that they do not brown. We call it poaching in oil; a great deal of the oil is not absorbed.

yield: 10 wedges

2 cups olive oil
2½ pounds thin-skinned potatoes, like Yukon Gold, peeled and sliced less than ⅛ inch thick
¾ pound onions, thinly sliced, slices cut in quarters

10 to 12 beaten eggs
Salt and freshly ground black pepper to taste

1. Heat the oil in a very large nonstick pan until it is very hot; add the potatoes and onions and reduce the heat to low so that the potatoes and onions cook but do not brown. It takes about 20 minutes.

2. As the potatoes cook, remove them from the oil with a slotted spoon and drain on paper towels. Blot well to remove as much oil as possible.

3. Gently mix the potatoes and onions with the eggs and season with the salt and pepper.

4. Heat some of the leftover oil, about 3 tablespoons, in a 10-inch pan until it is almost smoking; reduce the heat to medium and add the potato-onion-egg mixture. Move the spatula around the edge of the pan to keep the eggs from sticking to the edges and cook for about 5 minutes.

5. Flip the tortilla onto a plate and then slide it back into the pan to cook 4 or 5 minutes on the second side.

6. Turn out onto a serving dish and cool. Serve warm, at room temperature, or cold in wedges.

QUICHE LORRAINE

$\mathcal{W}$riting back in 1980 in *The New York Times*, Craig Claiborne said quiche first came to the attention of America around the mid-1950s. "Since then we have gone through what has amounted to the quiching of America," he said, from crabmeat to zucchini.

In the process, what most of us have forgotten is that quiche Lorraine does not contain cheese. This recipe for Quiche Lorraine is the original; the variation, perhaps more familiar to Americans, is made with cheese (page 24). It is possible to make ahead.

yield: 8 large pieces or 14 first-course slivers

6 ounces sliced bacon
6 eggs
2 cups light cream
2 cups heavy cream
1/2 teaspoon salt

Freshly ground black pepper to taste
1/4 teaspoon ground nutmeg
One unbaked 10-inch pie crust (page 25)
1 beaten egg yolk

1. Place a rack in the middle of the oven. Preheat the oven to 475 degrees. Place the bacon on a rack over a roasting pan and cook in the oven until it is medium-crisp (it should still bend), about 15 to 18 minutes, depending on the thickness of the bacon. Remove the bacon from the rack and pat it between paper towels to remove additional fat. Reduce the oven temperature to 375 degrees.

2. Beat the eggs until foamy; stir in the light and heavy creams, salt, pepper, and nutmeg. Chill for 30 minutes before using.

3. Brush the unbaked pie shell with the beaten yolk and prick it all over the bottom and sides with a fork. Pour in the filling.

4. Bake the quiche until it is almost set, 30 to 40 minutes. Watch the edges of the crust; if they get too brown, cover them with foil and continue baking. Cool the quiche on a rack and refrigerate, covered.

5. To serve, preheat the oven to 375 degrees. Bring the quiche to room temperature and bake 10 to 20 minutes, or until the center is set. Let stand for 15 minutes before cutting.

HELP NOTE: *If you don't want to partially bake the quiche, the filling and the shell can be made the day before and refrigerated, but the two cannot be combined until it is time to bake the quiche. Preheat the oven to 375 degrees and bring the shell and filling to room temperature before adding the filling to the shell. Bake for 45 minutes to an hour.*

Alternatively, preheat the oven to 400 degrees. Prick the shell all over, brush it with beaten egg yolk, and place a piece of wax paper in the shell; fill the shell with raw beans to keep it from puffing up. Bake the shell for 20 minutes and remove the beans and wax paper. Bake another 5 to 10 minutes until brown all over. Cool completely and cover but do not refrigerate.

The next day, preheat the oven to 375 degrees and bring the filling to room temperature. Pour the filling into the prebaked crust. Bake the quiche for 35 to 45 minutes. Purists claim the pie shell baked blind is crisper.

I use nitrite-free bacon; others recommend very thick bacon. I don't think the thickness makes that much difference, but the taste of the bacon does. Nitrite-free bacon is widely available, or see Sources, page 204. 🌿

QUICHE WITH CHEESE

*T*his is what most of us think of as the real quiche, but that recipe is on page 22. Here's how to make quiche the day before it is needed.

yield: 8 large pieces or 14 first-course slivers

6 ounces sliced bacon
5 eggs
2 cups light cream
1 cup heavy cream
2 cups grated aged Gruyère
½ cup grated Parmigiano-Reggiano

Salt and freshly ground black pepper
  to taste
¼ teaspoon nutmeg
One unbaked 10-inch pie crust (page 25)
1 beaten egg yolk

1. Place a rack in the middle of the oven. Preheat the oven to 475 degrees. Place the bacon on a rack over a roasting pan and cook in the oven until it is medium-crisp (it should still bend), about 15 to 18 minutes, depending on the thickness of the bacon. Remove the bacon from the rack and pat it between paper towels to remove additional fat. Reduce the oven temperature to 375 degrees.

2. Beat the eggs until foamy; stir in the light and heavy creams, the Gruyère and Parmigiano-Reggiano, salt, pepper, and nutmeg. Chill for 30 minutes before using.

3. Brush the unbaked pie shell with the beaten yolk and prick it all over the bottom and sides with a fork. Pour in the filling.

4. Bake the quiche until it is almost set, 30 to 40 minutes. Watch the edges of the crust; if they get too brown, cover them with foil and continue baking. Cool the quiche on a rack and refrigerate, covered.

5. To serve, preheat the oven to 375 degrees. Bring the quiche to room temperature and bake 10 to 20 minutes, or until the center is set. Let stand for 15 minutes before cutting.

HELP NOTE: Nitrite-free bacon is available in many stores, or see Sources, page 204. ❧

PIE CRUST

*T*his is Marion Cunningham's *pâte brisée*, so you can be certain it is foolproof. Marion, a dear friend and teacher, is *the* expert on baking and the author of the *Fannie Farmer Baking Book* (Random House, 1996), among many others.

yield: one 10-inch crust

1½ cups unbleached all-purpose flour
1½ tablespoons sugar
¼ teaspoon salt

12 tablespoons (1½ sticks) chilled
  unsalted butter
2 to 3 tablespoons ice water

1. Blend the flour, sugar, salt, and butter, using a pastry blender or your fingers. Add the water and shape the dough into a ball.

2. Flatten the ball; take small pieces of it and press them into the bottom and sides of a 10-inch pie plate, making sure the dough is not too thick at the bottom edge. Use the palm of your hand to flatten the dough. The pie shell is ready to fill. You do not need to flute the edge. ❦

MY MOTHER'S SOUR CREAM COFFEE CAKE

*N*ot the least of the charms of this simple coffee cake is the way the house smells while it is baking. When my mother baked this cake, it meant family was coming for a visit. I could hardly wait for the company or the cake.

yield: 8 to 12 servings

FILLING AND TOPPING
1 ½ cups finely chopped walnuts
6 tablespoons sugar
1 tablespoon ground cinnamon

CAKE
½ pound (2 sticks) unsalted butter, softened

1 ¼ cups sugar
2 ½ cups cake flour
1 teaspoon baking powder
1 teaspoon baking soda
¼ teaspoon salt
3 eggs
1 teaspoon pure vanilla extract
1 cup sour cream

1. Mix together the walnuts, sugar, and cinnamon and set aside.

2. Place a rack in the bottom third of the oven. Preheat the oven to 350 degrees. Grease a 9-inch springform or tube pan.

3. Using an electric mixer, cream the butter and sugar until very light in color.

4. Sift the flour and remeasure. Sift the flour again with the baking powder, baking soda, and salt. In a mixer set at low speed, alternately add the eggs and the flour mixture to the butter mixture.

5. Beat in the vanilla and sour cream until thoroughly blended.

6. Spoon half the batter into the prepared pan. Top with half the nut mixture, stirring as you add it to keep it mixed. Top with the remaining batter, smooth the top, and sprinkle with the remaining nut mixture.

7. Bake for 50 to 60 minutes until a cake tester inserted just off center comes out clean. Take the cake from the oven and cool in the pan on a wire rack for 10 minutes; remove the cake from the pan.

8. Serve warm or at room temperature.

VARIATION: *Susan Simon, better known as SueChef, who has helped me with several cookbooks, strongly suggests reducing the flour to 2 cups and adding ½ cup of wheat germ. The result is a very nutty flavor.*

HELP NOTE: *Refrigerate, or freeze up to a month, if desired, well covered. To serve, defrost and warm. It tastes best the second day.*

When baking, always test the cake at the earliest time. Oven temperatures vary, often by a lot, and it's easy to overbake a cake and dry it out.

It really is useful to own a good oven thermometer so you can test your oven, lowering or raising the heat if necessary. This is not an acute problem for roasting or braising, but it is a very serious problem for baking.

HORS D'OEUVRES
and APPETIZERS

PIMIENTO CHEESE SPREAD

$\mathcal{I}$ include this recipe with thanks to my Tennessee-born-and-bred friend Sara Mashek. The pimiento cheese spread of my childhood in New England came in a jar with a pry-off metal top, and once the spread was gone, the jar became a juice glass.

Considering the contents of those jars, I had no idea why people set such store by the stuff. But after I learned to make pimiento cheese spread with real Cheddar cheese and not processed cheese food spread (or whatever that stuff was), I understood. Sharp and sprightly, it takes the edge off your appetite.

Serve it on white toast; use it as a dip or as a stuffing for celery.

yield: 1 cup

One 4-ounce jar pimientos, drained and
finely chopped
¼ pound grated sharp Cheddar
¼ pound grated Monterey Jack
1 teaspoon dry mustard

Pinch cayenne pepper or more to taste
2 tablespoons mayonnaise
1 tablespoon white vinegar
Salt to taste

1. Mash the pimientos with the Cheddar and Monterey Jack, mustard, cayenne, mayonnaise, and vinegar. Season to taste with salt.

VARIATION: *Use ¼ pound finely chopped roasted red peppers in place of the pimiento.*

HELP NOTE: *Pimiento cheese can be made weeks in advance.*

COCKTAIL SAUCE FOR SHRIMP

This recipe is exactly the same one (if you don't count the oil) that I got from my mother fifty years ago. I've tasted dozens and dozens of versions at countless buffets, but this one is still the zestiest without burning your mouth. This recipe makes enough for about 1 pound of shrimp.

yield: 1 cup plus

⅓ cup chili sauce
⅓ cup catsup
3 tablespoons bottled grated horseradish
4 tablespoons lemon juice

2 teaspoons Worcestershire sauce
Shake or two hot pepper sauce
1 tablespoon oil, optional

1. Combine all the ingredients and mix well.

HELP NOTE: The oil takes some of the sharpness out of the sauce; if you prefer it spicy, don't use it. ❦

CHICKEN SALAD SPREAD

*U*se this to fill miniature baked tart shells or as a spread on toast rounds for hors d'oeuvres.

yield: 2 cups

2 cups ground roasted or poached chicken
3 tablespoons mayonnaise
2 tablespoons chopped unsalted cashews,
   toasted
1 stalk celery, finely chopped
2 tablespoons plain yogurt

1 ½ tablespoons finely chopped chutney
½ teaspoon curry powder
¼ teaspoon ground coriander
1 tablespoon lemon juice
Salt and freshly ground black pepper
   to taste

1. Combine all the ingredients and mix well. Refrigerate, if desired, for several hours or up to a day to blend the flavors.

HELP NOTE: *Leftover turkey? Here's a delicious way to use it up without anyone's making snide comments.*

The filling also makes a great sandwich; use a little more mayo.

For the streamlined version, use light mayonnaise. 🌾

HOMEMADE CALIFORNIA DIP

I don't care how sophisticated your tastes are; at some point in your life you ate sour cream combined with dried onion soup mix as a dip for potato chips. Now that dip is back in a homemade version in which onion, not salt, is the main flavoring agent.

yield: 2 cups

6 tablespoons flavorless vegetable oil, such as canola
3 cups finely minced onions
1 teaspoon sugar
½ teaspoon Worcestershire sauce
1 tablespoon lemon juice
3 cups sour cream
Salt to taste

1. Heat the oil on medium-high heat in a large skillet that does *not* have a non-stick surface.

2. Brown the onions, stirring often. Watch carefully so that they do not burn. As they cook add the sugar.

3. When they are golden, cover, reduce the heat, and cook another 10 minutes, stirring often.

4. Remove the onions to a plate covered with paper towels and blot with additional towels to get rid of some of the fat. (Several blots will be necessary.)

5. Mix the onions with the Worcestershire, lemon juice, sour cream, and salt to taste. Cover and chill for several hours or overnight. Serve with potato chips.

HELP NOTE: *To cut the onions easily, slice them very finely on a mandoline and then chop. You don't have to spend a fortune on a French mandoline; there is an excellent Japanese version, which is far less expensive and is handy for many cutting chores.* ❦

HUMMUS

The full name of this recipe is *hummus bi tahini*. Tahini is a paste made of sesame seeds and oil, an important ingredient in Middle Eastern cooking. A decade or more ago hummus became an American hors d'oeuvre, so popular that ready-made hummus is available in the refrigerated section of many ordinary supermarkets.

I know a lot of people who make dinner out of it when they come home late from work.

yield: 1⅓ cups

3 cloves garlic
One 15-ounce can garbanzos or
   chickpeas, rinsed and drained
5 tablespoons tahini (sesame paste)
2 tablespoons water
2 tablespoons extra virgin olive oil
6 tablespoons lemon juice
1 teaspoon ground cumin
Cayenne pepper to taste, optional
Salt to taste

FOR GARNISH
2 tablespoons minced fresh parsley
Lemon wedges, Greek olives, and
   additional olive oil

1 package pita breads

1. With the food processor running, put the garlic through the feed tube and process until minced.

2. Add the garbanzos, tahini, water, olive oil, lemon juice, cumin, and cayenne, if using, and process until the mixture is smooth. Season with the salt. Refrigerate to blend the flavors for at least a couple of hours but up to 2 days, if desired.

3. To serve, return the hummus to room temperature. Sprinkle with the parsley and decorate with the lemon wedges, olives, and a drizzle of additional olive oil, if desired. Serve with warm pita wedges.

HELP NOTE: The texture should be that of a spread. Adding cayenne is not typical, but it gives a nice kick. 🌿

DEVILED EGGS

Is any picnic complete without stuffed eggs?

yield: 12 stuffed egg halves

6 eggs
2 teaspoons Dijon mustard
2 teaspoons finely grated onion
5 tablespoons mayonnaise (approximately)

I teaspoon curry powder, optional
Salt and freshly ground black pepper
   to taste
Parsley for garnish, optional

1. Hard-cook the eggs: Place them in a pot of cold water and bring the water to a boil. Boil for 3 minutes, gently stirring the eggs often so that the yolks are centered. Remove the pot from the heat and allow the eggs to sit in the water, covered, for 20 minutes. Run the eggs under cold water until they are cooled.

2. Shell the eggs and cut them in half lengthwise. Remove the yolks and in a small bowl mash the yolks together with the mustard, onion, mayonnaise, curry powder, if using, plus salt and pepper to taste. The mixture should be creamy.

3. Stuff the whites with the mashed yolk mixture. If you want to make them pretty you can pipe the mixture through a pastry tube; otherwise, decorate with fork tines. Cover and chill. Top with a sprig of parsley, if desired.

VARIATIONS: *For Shrimp-Stuffed Eggs, mix 3 tablespoons of finely minced cooked shrimp into the yolk mixture.*

For Ham-Stuffed Eggs, mix 1 to 2 tablespoons of finely chopped ham into the yolk mixture, or use honey mustard in place of Dijon.

HELP NOTE: *The only commercial mayonnaise to use is Hellmann's (called Best Foods west of the Rockies). If you're calorie-conscious, light mayonnaise works well here because the strong flavors of the seasonings mask the flavor of the mayonnaise.*

CHEESE PECAN WAFERS

*S*ome version or other of these cheese wafers has been part of my repertoire for forty years. I love them because they freeze so well (either before or after baking) and defrost so quickly. They are too good to be called an emergency hors d'oeuvre, but they fit the bill.

yield: 48 wafers

1 pound extra-sharp white Cheddar, grated

16 tablespoons (2 sticks) unsalted butter, softened

2 cups unbleached all-purpose flour

1 cup finely chopped pecans

1/8 teaspoon or more cayenne pepper

1. Cream the Cheddar and butter until thoroughly mixed, using an electric mixer or a food processor.

2. Add the flour, pecans, and cayenne and mix thoroughly. Shape the dough into rolls 1 inch in diameter by rolling the dough between sheets of wax paper. Wrap the rolls in wax paper or plastic and place in the freezer for 30 minutes or so, until quite firm.

3. Position the rack in the middle of the oven and preheat the oven to 400 degrees. Slice the rolls into 1/3-inch-thick slices and place them on ungreased cookie sheets about 1/2 inch apart. Bake 10 to 15 minutes until light brown on the bottom.

HELP NOTE: *Freezing the dough makes it much easier to cut neatly. If you freeze the dough for more than 30 minutes, let it stand at room temperature for about 10 minutes before slicing. Store the wafers in a tightly covered container for several days or freeze, well wrapped in foil. The dough can be frozen for several weeks, well wrapped in foil.* ❦

To order well-aged cheese, see Sources, page 203.

ANNE AMERNICK'S CHEESE PUFF PASTRY STRIPS

Anne Amernick, once an assistant pastry chef at the White House, is considered one of the finest bakers in Washington, D.C. She is famous for her wedding cakes. Anne and another alumnus of the White House kitchen, Frank Ruta, who was a chef there, are owners of Palena, a marvelous small restaurant in Washington where these puffs are served before dinner. The puffs are also available at Anne's pastry shop, Amernick's, in Washington, D.C.

The flakiness of the puff pastry, the intensity and richness of the two cheeses, the toasty sweetness and added crunch of the nuts combine to produce bet-you-can't-eat-just-one cheese strips.

yield: 5 to 7 dozen strips

I pound puff pastry dough, purchased or homemade

2 cups blanched and sliced almonds

2 cups grated Parmigiano-Reggiano and aged Gouda mixture

I beaten egg

1. If the dough is frozen, defrost it. In a bowl, blend the almonds and Parmigiano-Reggiano and Gouda.

2. Place the dough on a well-floured board. Flour the top of the dough and turn it over.

3. Flour the top of the dough; flour the rolling pin and roll out dough on heavily floured board to fit a baking sheet either about 14 by 16 inches or 12 by 17 inches.

4. Roll the dough onto the rolling pin and unroll onto a baking sheet. Brush the dough with the beaten egg and sprinkle the nut-cheese mixture evenly over the dough. Cut the dough into approximately 4-inch strips and then cut the strips into ¾-inch strips. Refrigerate for 30 minutes.

5. Place a rack in the middle of the oven and preheat the oven to 375 degrees. Bake the strips for 20 to 25 minutes. Remove from oven and cool.

6. Store in a tightly covered container.

HELP NOTE: *The strips can be refreshed in a 350-degree oven for a few minutes, if needed.*

Strips can be frozen. Reheat at 350 degrees for about 7 minutes, or until warm.

Anne uses a combination of cheeses for her puffs, depending on what is in Palena's refrigerator. Sometimes it's aged goat cheese and Manchego. My favorite blend is one-half Parmigiano-Reggiano and one-half aged Gouda.

Buy your puff pastry from a local bakery or on-line; see Sources, page 204.

It puffs much better than the more famous national brand of puff pastry dough that also makes frozen pastries and cakes. ❦

COLD SESAME NOODLES

I don't know if sesame noodles are comfort food for the Chinese, but I can't think of many dishes that make me feel as good.

yield: 6 first-course servings

12 ounces Chinese noodles, preferably fresh
1 tablespoon Asian sesame oil
5 tablespoons brewed tea or water
3 tablespoons soy sauce
3 tablespoons Asian sesame paste
1 ½ tablespoons peanut oil
1 ½ tablespoons dry sherry

1 tablespoon red wine vinegar
1 ½ teaspoons sugar
3 cloves garlic, crushed
1 tablespoon coarsely grated fresh ginger
2 teaspoons hot chili oil
1 tablespoon black sesame seeds, optional
Thinly sliced green onions for garnish

1. Cook the noodles according to package directions in boiling water, 2 to 4 minutes. Do not overcook. Drain well and toss with the sesame oil.

2. Combine the remaining ingredients except green onions in food processor and process to blend thoroughly.

3. Mix the noodles with the sesame dressing. Let cool to room temperature and sprinkle with the sliced green onions.

WINE: *Riesling*

HELP NOTE: Chinese noodles, Asian sesame oil, sesame paste, hot chili oil, and black sesame seeds are available at Asian markets, some supermarkets, and on-line (see Sources, page 203), but if it is impossible to find them, here are some substitutes: Creamy unsweetened peanut butter can be used in place of the sesame paste. If fresh Chinese noodles are not available, substitute fresh Italian linguine. Don't substitute Middle Eastern tahini or sesame paste or Middle Eastern sesame oil for the Asian. Asian sesame paste and oil are toasted; Middle Eastern is not. 🌱

QUESADILLAS

*T*his may not be the original comfort food of the Tex-Mex kitchen, but it is delicious and so easy to prepare. I am using this recipe to represent flavors of the cooking that has swept through this country from the West and Southwest, making salsa an even bigger seller than catsup. You can serve these in wedges as an hors d'oeuvre or snack, or as a sandwich for lunch or light dinner.

yield: 36 to 48 wedges

6 flour tortillas (7 to 8 inches in diameter)
3 cups coarsely grated Monterey Jack (8 ounces)
3 roasted red and/or yellow bell peppers, thinly sliced, slices cut in half

1 large or 2 small mangoes, ripe but still quite firm, peeled and cut in small dice
2 green onions, white and some of light green finely cut
1 small jalapeño, seeded and minced

1. Heat a griddle or stove-top grill over medium heat.

2. Top half of each tortilla with ½ cup Monterey Jack, half of a pepper, one-sixth of the mango(es), one-sixth of the green onions, and jalapeño to taste.

3. Place as many tortillas as will fit on the griddle. Cook the tortillas about 20 seconds, then fold over the uncovered half, press down, and flip the folded tortilla. Brown on second side about 1 minute or until the cheese is melted.

4. Remove the quesadillas, cut in thirds or quarters, and serve immediately.

5. Repeat until all the tortillas are used.

HELP NOTE: *The two essentials for quesadillas are tortillas and cheese, preferably Monterey Jack. After that it seems that anything goes, including Brie or Camembert instead of Monterey Jack. Other fillings include roasted long green mild chiles and Monterey Jack; black beans, goat cheese, and tomato; shrimp or crabmeat with the peppers and mangoes. I've tasted quesadillas filled with crabmeat and mayonnaise, and they are outstanding. The quesadillas are wonderful with guacamole on the side, and they can be prepared equally well with whole-wheat tortillas.* ❧

MOLLIE DICKENSON'S GUACAMOLE TOSTADOS

*M*y friend Mollie Dickenson once brought this to a cooperative dinner party. It disappeared so quickly that she achieved instant fame, and now she is always asked to bring this. It may not be recognizable as comfort food to those of us brought up on the East Coast or in the middle of the country, where the only way we ever ate an avocado was with shrimp. But the ingredients in this must have been comfort food early on in the West and Southwest, where Mexican influences are as much a part of the landscape as baked beans are in New England.

yield: 16 servings

I cup dried pinto beans (see Help Note, page 43)
¾ cup chopped onion
I large clove garlic, minced
1½ teaspoons ground cumin
2½ tablespoons mild chili powder
I tablespoon white wine vinegar
4 tablespoons (½ stick) unsalted butter, softened
3 ounces tomato paste
¼ teaspoon ground coriander seed
8 drops hot pepper sauce

Salt and freshly ground black pepper to taste
2 medium or large ripe avocados
2 tablespoons lemon juice
I cup sour cream
2 large ripe tomatoes, chopped
¾ cup chopped green onions
I cup chopped pitted black olives
2 cups coarsely grated sharp white Cheddar
2/3 cup coarsely chopped fresh cilantro
Good-quality tortilla chips

1. To prepare the beans, cover them with water and soak overnight. Alternatively, cover them with water and bring to a boil; boil for 2 minutes and allow the beans to sit in the hot water for 1 hour. Drain off the soaking water. Cover the beans with fresh water, and bring to a boil. Add ½ cup chopped onion, garlic, and ½ teaspoon of the cumin. Cover and simmer until beans are tender, about an hour. Stir occasionally. Drain.

2. Place the beans in a food processor with ¾ teaspoon of the cumin, 1½ tablespoons of the chili powder, vinegar, butter, tomato paste, coriander, and hot pepper sauce. Process until mixture is smooth. Adjust the seasoning and add salt and pepper to taste.

3. Peel the avocados and mash coarsely with lemon juice and salt and pepper to taste.

4. Mix the sour cream with the remaining 1 tablespoon chili powder and ¼ teaspoon cumin.

5. Spread the bean mixture in a shallow serving dish. Top with the mashed avocados, then the sour cream mixture. Refrigerate for at least 4 hours, or overnight, if desired. Up to an hour before serving, sprinkle the tomatoes evenly over the sour cream. Sprinkle with the green onions, olives, and Cheddar, and top with the cilantro.

6. Serve with tortilla chips.

HELP NOTE: *You can substitute 3 cups of canned beans, thoroughly rinsed and drained, for the fresh-cooked beans, but add the other ingredients cooked with the beans to the recipe. Frankly, Mollie Dickenson uses canned beans in her recipe.*

This recipe is best prepared a day or even two ahead. Just don't add the tomatoes, green onions, olives, cheese, and cilantro until you're ready to serve.

Because there are so many flavors in this dish, you can use reduced-fat sour cream, and trust me, no one will know the difference. ❦

MARYLAND CRAB CAKES

I knew very little about crabs until I moved to Washington, D.C., in 1959. It was love at first sight. These crab cakes are made after the fashion of the famous Faidley's Seafood market in the equally famous Lexington Market in Baltimore. The theory there is that less is more. The crab cakes have no onion, no green pepper, and absolutely no bread crumbs. Bread crumbs are too heavy; cracker crumbs are used instead.

Maybe you have to live in this part of the country to realize how much better crab cakes are made this way compared to some versions that have more of everything than crab. And it is so important to have lump crab so that there are nice big sweet chunks to bite into. You can serve a single crab cake as an appetizer, or two (or more) as a main course.

yield: 8 cakes

1 lightly beaten egg	1 cup crushed saltines
½ cup mayonnaise	1 pound fresh lump crabmeat
1 tablespoon Dijon mustard	Salt to taste, optional
1 tablespoon Worcestershire sauce	4 tablespoons neutral-flavored vegetable
½ teaspoon hot pepper sauce	oil, such as canola

1. Mix together the egg, mayonnaise, mustard, Worcestershire, and hot pepper sauce in a bowl large enough to hold all the ingredients.

2. Finely crush the saltines between two pieces of wax paper with a rolling pin. Fold the crushed crackers into the mayonnaise mixture.

3. Pick over the crabmeat to remove bits of shell or cartilage. Fold the crabmeat into the mayonnaise mixture and season with salt, if desired. Gently shape into 8 crab cakes, handling as little as possible. Refrigerate, covered, if desired.

4. To serve, heat the oil in a pan large enough to hold the crab cakes and sauté over medium heat, about 3 minutes on each side, until golden brown.

WINE: *Chardonnay, Sauvignon Blanc, or Riesling*

HELP NOTE: *A lemon wedge served as an accompaniment is acceptable, but no tartar sauce, please.*

The quality of the crabmeat is extremely important. It is difficult to get unpasteurized crabmeat outside the mid-Atlantic states and Southeast, but it is sweeter. I've seen crab cakes made with just about every other kind of crab, but to me none is as good as blue crab. People in the Northwest and in the South will have other ideas.

For some in this area of the country, Old Bay seasoning is critical, but to me it masks the sweetness of the crab.

Some people coat the crab cakes in bread crumbs; I think it makes them taste drier. I also think sautéing brings out the delicate flavor better than deep-fat frying.

I've tried sautéing the crab cakes in oil and in butter; there is a slight difference in taste but it's very small, and with oil there is less chance of burning the fat.

Above all, fold the crab gently into the other ingredients; do not work the meat or it will break up. Do not flatten down the crab cakes; mold them gently into a cake shape.

For a streamlined version, light mayonnaise works as well as the regular kind. ❦

SOUPS, SANDWICHES, *and* SALADS

MY MOTHER'S CHICKEN SOUP

Chicken soup "is the most universal cure-all," writes Ken Hom in *Ken Hom's East Meets West Cuisine* (Simon & Schuster, 1987). It's as important in Chinese cuisine as it is in Jewish, Vietnamese, Hungarian, Greek, and Italian.

And, yes, chicken soup *is* good for colds. Three physicians at The Mount Sinai Medical Center in Miami Beach performed an experiment and discovered that drinking hot chicken soup is helpful for a stuffy nose. It's the steam!

yield: 6 cups

3 to 4 pounds chicken parts (see Help
   Note below)
3 carrots, washed
3 stalks celery, washed and cut in thirds
I large sliced onion
4 sprigs parsley
6 peppercorns

I sprig thyme
I sprig rosemary
I sage leaf
Salt and finely ground black pepper
   to taste
6 cups water

1. Combine all the ingredients in a large pot. Cover and bring to a boil. Reduce the heat and simmer for 2 hours, stirring occasionally. Strain the broth through a cheesecloth-lined strainer. Chill for several hours.

2. Remove the soup from the refrigerator and skim the fat from the soup. Reheat and serve.

HELP NOTE: *You can use any combination of chicken parts in this recipe.*

The soup will keep a couple of days in the refrigerator or frozen for at least a month.

To make an elegant presentation, float strips of cooked mushrooms on the soup; to make it homey, stir in cooked fine egg noodles.

And, of course, there are Matzo Balls. See page 50 for the recipe.

MATZO BALLS

*O*ne test of a fine Jewish cook was her matzo balls: Those who made heavy ones were laughed at; those who made light, feathery ones were admired (at least when I was growing up). My mother's were much admired.

But not everyone wants light matzo balls, as I found out recently at a friend's Passover seder. Those who grew up with "firm" matzo balls (what my family disparagingly called "sinkers") thought mine were too light. "Not chewy enough," said one from the sinker side.

yield: 14 to 16 large matzo balls

1 cup matzo meal	4 tablespoons water
4 beaten eggs	1 ½ to 2 teaspoons salt
4 tablespoons oil or chicken fat	¼ cup finely chopped chives, optional

1. Combine all the ingredients and refrigerate for 40 minutes.

2. Bring a large pot of salted water to a boil.

3. With wet hands, shape the mixture into balls 1 inch in diameter, or, if you desire something more "elegant," shape the mixture into balls about the size of your thumb. Drop them into boiling water, cover, and simmer them for 20 minutes, the smaller ones for 10 minutes. Drain and refrigerate until ready to serve, or freeze in the chicken soup for up to a month.

4. To serve, reheat the matzo balls gently in chicken soup (page 49).

VARIATIONS: *Mix 1 tablespoon finely chopped parsley or 1 tablespoon finely chopped dill with the other ingredients.*

HELP NOTE: *If the balls are frozen, to serve, defrost and bring to a boil in the chicken soup.* ❧

CHINESE EGG DROP SOUP

*E*gg drop soup is comfort food not only for the Chinese but also for millions of Americans whose first taste of ethnic food was Chinese.

Looking at recipes for the soup shows a culinary evolution in this country that brings a smile to my face. The earliest recipe I have calls for thickening the soup with cornstarch, using canned chicken broth, and seasoning it with MSG. Times have changed.

The addition of the sherry and toasted sesame oil, I confess, is a contemporary permutation, but the subtle hint of those flavors is perfectly delicious.

yield: 6 cups

6 cups Chicken Soup (page 49)
One ¼-inch-thick slice fresh ginger
3 lightly beaten eggs
2 teaspoons dry sherry

3 green onions, white and light green part,
   finely chopped
Toasted or Asian sesame oil for garnish

1. Make the chicken soup with a slice of ginger, or add a slice of ginger to the soup when you reheat it. Bring the soup to a boil. Remove the ginger and discard.

2. Whisk the eggs with the sherry. Slowly pour the eggs into the boiling soup in a stream, stirring back and forth (not around) with a pair of chopsticks until all of the eggs have been added. Remove the soup from the heat and allow to sit for 30 seconds.

3. Ladle the soup into bowls, top each serving with some of the green onions, and drizzle a few drops of the sesame oil on the top of each bowl.

HELP NOTE: *Toasted or Asian sesame oil tastes different from Middle Eastern sesame oil. Asian is made from toasted sesame seeds.* ❦

ONION SOUP

*M*ost of what passes for onion soup in this country would not meet the taste test. Onion soup should have a deeply, richly flavored stock, chock-a-block with onions and a generous layer of cheese on top.

yield: 4 servings as a main dish or 8 servings as a first course

3 tablespoons unsalted butter
1 tablespoon olive oil, PLUS oil for brushing
1½ pounds onions, thinly sliced
¼ teaspoon sugar
1 tablespoon flour
2 quarts good-quality strong beef stock
1 cup dry white wine

Salt and freshly ground black pepper
 to taste
14 to 18 1-inch-thick slices French
 bread
2 cups coarsely grated aged Gruyère
 (about 6 ounces)
4 tablespoons cognac, optional

1. Heat the butter and 1 tablespoon olive oil in a heavy-bottomed pot over low heat. Add the onions and cook, covered, until they are soft, about 15 minutes.

2. Uncover the pot and raise the heat to medium; stir in the sugar (which helps the browning process), and sauté the onions until they turn a deep golden color. Stir often; scrape the bottom and watch carefully, especially at the end, so that they don't burn. Adjust the heat as necessary. Cook about 30 minutes.

3. Stir in the flour to blend well. Remove the pot from the heat and stir in the beef stock and wine. Season with the salt and pepper and bring to boil. Reduce the heat and simmer 30 minutes. Refrigerate, if desired.

4. To serve, preheat the oven to 325 degrees. Arrange the bread slices on a cookie sheet and bake for about 30 minutes, until the slices are dry and crisp. Brush the slices with oil on both sides halfway through the toasting and turn over. Remove the bread and raise the oven temperature to 425 degrees.

5. Bring the soup to a boil. Stir in ⅓ cup of the Gruyère and the 4 tablespoons of cognac, if using, and pour the soup into an ovenproof tureen or individual oven-proof bowls. Arrange the toasts on top of the soup and sprinkle the remaining Gruyère generously over the slices. Place the bowl(s) in the oven and bake until the cheese and bread are brown and crusty, about 10 minutes Serve piping hot.

HELP NOTE: *After step 3, the soup can be refrigerated or frozen for up to a month, if desired. To finish, continue with the recipe.*

Don't worry about the skin that forms on top of the soup; just stir it back in.

Writing in the 1970s, both Julia Child and Craig Claiborne said canned bouillon or half bouillon and half water could be used instead of stock. Well, their books are old and you can buy very good stock now. It isn't cheap, but it is full-bodied and flavorful.

For a complete meal, serve a large salad after. ❦

CORN, POTATO, AND BACON CHOWDER

*I*f you like this, you can thank Madeleine Kamman, the brilliant French cooking teacher. She came for lunch to the house in Vermont during summer 2002 and liked the chowder as much as she had liked the beet and cucumber soups a couple of years before. She said it should definitely be in the book.

This soup is hearty but says summer at the same time; it is perfect for those days and nights when the corn is still sweet but there is a chill in the air.

It's the smokiness from the bacon, the sweetness of the fresh corn, the touch of heat from the cayenne, and the herbaceous flavor from the thyme that set this soup apart. Cream doesn't hurt either.

yield: 8 to 10 servings

8 strips nitrite-free bacon (see Sources, page 204)

3 cups chopped onions

½ teaspoon cayenne pepper

2 large cloves garlic, minced

1 bay leaf

1 tablespoon fresh thyme leaves, PLUS fresh thyme tops for garnish

3 cups peeled potatoes, cut in ½-inch dice

8 cups good-quality chicken stock

2 cups heavy cream

6 cups fresh corn kernels (8 to 10 large ears of corn)

Salt and freshly ground black pepper to taste

1. Cut the bacon in small pieces and sauté until it is crisp.

2. Add the onions and cayenne and sauté until the onions are soft and beginning to color.

3. Add the garlic, bay leaf, thyme leaves, potatoes, and chicken stock and bring to a boil. Cook, uncovered, until the potatoes are tender, 10 to 15 minutes.

4. Add the cream and corn, and cook until the cream is almost at the boiling point, just a couple of minutes, which is long enough to cook corn. Season with salt and pepper. Discard the bay leaf. Garnish with the fresh thyme tops.

HELP NOTE: This chowder may be prepared ahead through step 3, to the point where the potatoes are cooked. Refrigerate and when ready to serve, reheat; add the cream and corn and continue.

Leftover chowder can be reheated; there are those who actually think it is better the second day.

If you long for this chowder on a cold winter day, you can use frozen corn kernels.

NEW ENGLAND CLAM CHOWDER

*A*s a native New Englander, to me there is only one clam chowder. Everything else is soup with clams in it.

yield: about 8 cups

1 large onion, chopped
3 tablespoons butter or 2 tablespoons oil
　and 1 tablespoon butter
1½ cups clam juice
2 medium large new potatoes, scrubbed
　and cut into ½-inch dice
1 bay leaf
1 teaspoon chopped fresh thyme

2 cups heavy cream (see Help Note
　below)
½ cup milk
1 tablespoon flour
1½ pints shucked clams
Salt and freshly ground black pepper
　to taste
Chopped fresh parsley for garnish

1. Sauté the onion in the butter over medium-high heat until translucent.

2. Add the clam juice, potatoes, bay leaf, and thyme and bring to a boil. Simmer until the potatoes are tender, 10 to 15 minutes.

3. Add the cream and bring to a simmer. Stir a little of the milk into the flour to make a paste. Add the paste to the remaining milk and stir into the soup.

4. Reduce the heat until it is as low as possible and add the clams for just a few minutes until the clams are cooked. Don't overcook the clams. Discard the bay leaf. The chowder should be thick. Season with salt and pepper and serve sprinkled with parsley.

HELP NOTE: Saltines, oyster crackers, or common crackers are the usual accompaniment to chowder.

If you don't want to use heavy cream you could substitute 2 cups half-and-half and ½ cup milk, or 2 cups milk and ½ cup half-and-half. Increase the amount of flour to 2 tablespoons. The flour is essential; otherwise, the soup will curdle. ❦

CREAM OF TOMATO SOUP

I had no intention of including a tomato soup in this book, but when so many people mentioned tomato soup in the same breath as toasted cheese sandwiches, the die was cast. It's not Campbell's; it's better.

yield: 6½ cups

Three 28-ounce cans whole tomatoes
   packed in liquid, drained, liquid reserved
2 tablespoons unsalted butter
1 cup finely chopped onion
2 tablespoons flour
2 cups good-quality chicken stock or broth

¼ cup full-bodied dry white wine
1 tablespoon tomato paste
1 tablespoon lemon juice
1 tablespoon sugar
Salt to taste
¾ cup heavy cream

1. Place the oven rack in the upper third of the oven. Preheat the oven to 450 degrees. Line a jelly roll pan or rimmed cookie sheet with foil.

2. Put the tomatoes from two cans in a single layer on the pan. Roast the tomatoes for 30 minutes. Remove them from the sheet and peel off any foil; cut off any browned parts. Cut each tomato in half.

3. Melt the butter in a heavy-bottomed pot. Sauté the onion over medium heat for about 10 minutes, until the onion is soft. Remove the pan from the heat and stir in the flour. Return the pan to medium heat and whisk in the chicken stock. Stir in 2 cups of the reserved tomato liquid, the wine, tomato paste, lemon juice, sugar, and roasted tomatoes. Bring to a boil, reduce the heat, and simmer for 10 minutes to blend, stirring occasionally.

4. Remove the tomatoes from the soup, place them in a food processor with some of the liquid, and puree. Set them aside and puree the rest of the mixture; combine in a pot and season with salt.

5. Warm the soup over low heat. Add the cream and stir to blend.

6. Serve hot.

HELP NOTE: *Save the tomatoes from the third can for another use.*
   The soup can be made ahead and refrigerated for up to 2 days. Reheat it over low heat; do not boil.
   Serve with a Toasted Cheese Sandwich (page 57). 🌿

TOASTED CHEESE SANDWICHES

I knew from the beginning exactly what I wanted: sandwiches sautéed in a pan, grilled, not broiled. I also knew the bread had to be thin and white, not as flimsy as Wonder Bread; something of a little higher quality, but no crusty crusts. And I knew the sandwiches had to be weighted down with a brick or something similar while they were browning in the butter that had been spread on the outside of each slice.

But then I tested panini grills for *The New York Times*. I even tried using my fifty-year-old waffle iron to make them. I loved those sandwiches, because the machines compress the bread so nicely and the cheese oozes out. If you have a panini grill or a waffle iron, grill your sandwiches that way.

What goes inside is the real version of American cheese: Cheddar, the sharper the better (see Sources, page 203), removed from a big piece with a cheese slicer. The cheese has to be thick enough not to disappear into the bread as it melts, but not so thick it doesn't melt completely as the bread browns. I'd say about a ⅛-inch-thick slice, or a little more, is about right. The cheese can also be grated. You could also use any sharply flavored cheese that melts easily. I love Boursin with bacon, and Cheddar with ham, and Gouda with Dijon mustard and a little hot pepper.

I tried the sandwiches plain and with tomato slices, and loved both. In a pan, weighted; in a panini grill; in a waffle iron.

Whatever the combination, whatever the means of cooking, do it slowly.

Serve with Cream of Tomato Soup, of course (page 56).

CHILLED BEET AND CUCUMBER SOUPS

$\mathcal{M}$adeleine Kamman, the cookbook author, understands as well as anyone alive how food works, and she can explain everything in person or in print. She was coming to dinner at our house in Vermont. My friend and fellow food writer Julian Armstrong, of the *Montreal Gazette*, knew that we had to make a non-French meal. No sense trying to compete with the master!

The first course was a pairing of beet and cucumber soups. It was such a success that Madeleine asked to take home the leftovers.

Each of these soups stands on its own but never looks as good as when the two are served side by side in a bowl (see Help Note, page 59).

I remember these two very good soups from my childhood; I liked neither of them at the time. Now I find them delightfully refreshing on a hot summer day.

yield: 3 servings

BEET SOUP

4 medium beets	1 cup good-quality chicken stock, or more
1 tablespoon balsamic vinegar	Pinch salt
1 tablespoon rice wine vinegar	Freshly ground black pepper to taste
½ teaspoon sugar	1½ teaspoons chopped fresh mint leaves

1. Peel and halve or quarter the beets and place in a medium saucepan with water to cover. Bring to a boil, reduce the heat, and simmer about 30 minutes, until the beets are tender but still firm. Drain and cool the beets.

2. Chop the beets roughly and place some in the blender with the vinegars, sugar, and some of the stock. Puree the beets and place in a nonreactive container. Repeat with the remaining beets and stock until all are pureed. If the mixture is too thick, add more stock. Season to taste with salt and pepper. Cover the container, and refrigerate for at least 2 hours or overnight.

3. To serve, chop the mint and place some in the center of each bowl (see Help Note, page 59).

CUCUMBER SOUP

6 small Kirby cucumbers
1 1/4 cups sour cream
3/4 cup plain whole-milk yogurt
1 1/2 tablespoons lemon juice, or more

Dash salt
White pepper to taste
1 1/2 teaspoons chopped fresh mint leaves

1. Wash but do not peel the cucumbers. Coarsely chop the cucumbers and place some of them in the blender with some of the sour cream, some of the yogurt, and the lemon juice. Puree, and transfer the mixture to a nonreactive container. Repeat with the remaining cucumbers, sour cream, and yogurt.

2. Season with the salt and pepper and add more lemon juice, if needed. Cover and chill for at least 2 hours or overnight.

3. To serve, chop the mint and sprinkle some in the middle of each bowl.

HELP NOTE: *Each soup serves only three, but when combined they serve six. Pour each soup into a pitcher. Pour the soups into rimmed soup bowls simultaneously from each side so that you have a bowl that is half ruby red and half pale green; place the chopped mint in the middle.*

The amount of water in cucumbers varies; the resulting soup will be thinner or thicker depending on the water content of your vegetables. Because you want the two soups to be of similar consistency it may be necessary to add more sour cream to the cucumber soup to thicken it or yogurt to thin it.

If you want a streamlined version of the cucumber soup, you can use reduced-fat sour cream and nonfat yogurt; no one will ever know, but reduce the amounts of yogurt and sour cream if using in combination with beet soup so the thickness will be the same. ❦

MUSHROOM BARLEY SOUP

$\mathcal{M}$y mother made this soup all the time in the winter. She used dried mushrooms that came in a little cellophane package from somewhere in the middle of Europe, not porcini. She didn't use fresh cremini, shiitake, or portobellos but what were called button mushrooms in those days, the plain white ones.

I always remember feeling full after eating this soup.

yield: 6 or 7 cups

1/3 cup dried mushrooms, such as
   porcini
1 cup hot water
2 tablespoons oil
1 medium onion, diced
1 medium carrot, diced
2 cloves garlic, minced
1/2 pound white mushrooms, washed,
   trimmed, and coarsely cut

1/2 pound shiitake, cremini, portobello, or
   other mushrooms, washed, trimmed, and
   coarsely cut
1/2 cup pearled barley
6 cups good-quality beef broth or stock
3 tablespoons dry sherry
Salt and freshly ground black pepper
   to taste
1 tablespoon wine vinegar

1. Cover the dried mushrooms with the hot water and set aside for 20 minutes. Drain, reserving the liquid, and finely chop the mushrooms.

2. Heat the oil in a heavy-bottomed deep pot. Sauté the onion and carrot in the oil over medium heat until the onion begins to color. Add the garlic and sauté for 30 seconds. Add the fresh mushrooms and sauté for about 5 minutes, until the mushrooms soften and begin to release their liquid.

3. Raise the heat, add the barley, and sauté until it begins to color slightly. Add the broth and sherry. Strain the mushroom soaking liquid through a fine strainer and add to the pot along with the reconstituted mushrooms. Season with salt and pepper and simmer for about 40 minutes, until the barley is tender.

4. Stir in the wine vinegar; adjust the seasonings and serve.

HELP NOTE: *The soup is even better if refrigerated overnight. The soup can be refrigerated for up to 3 days or frozen for a month. Reheat to serve.*

The taste of this soup begins with the stock; the better the stock tastes the better everything else will. Today at many specialty markets, you can buy high-quality beef stock that is rich and full-bodied without being salted to a fare-thee-well.

It's not traditional, but adding wine vinegar to the soup gives it a sparkle. 🌿

THE PERFECT BLT

This sandwich is best made when tomatoes are at their peak, but I've cheated in winter by using those cherry tomatoes that come with stems on. It's okay when you are desperate for a BLT fix.

I cook the bacon on a rack over a jelly roll pan at 450 degrees in the middle of the oven until the bacon is very brown but not completely crisp. You have to choose the most flavorful bacon; I recommend Applegate Farms of Branchburg, New Jersey, and Yorkshire Farms of Swedesboro, New Jersey, because their products have an excellent bacon taste and are nitrite-free (see Sources, page 204).

The lettuce of choice is the soft part of romaine leaves. The bread is white with a good crust—something from a bakery, not the supermarket. And the mayonnaise is Hellmann's (or Best Foods) and plenty of it.

TUNA SANDWICH

*W*e never called these tuna sandwiches; they were always tuna *fish* sandwiches.

yield: 2 sandwiches

One 6- or 7-ounce can albacore tuna in oil
1 hard-cooked egg, finely chopped
2 tablespoons sweet pickle relish
4 teaspoons finely chopped celery
4 tablespoons mayonnaise
2 teaspoons lemon juice

Salt and freshly ground black pepper
  to taste
2 leaves lettuce
4 slices good soft white bread
2 to 4 slices tomato, optional

1. Drain the tuna and flake (use your fingers). Add the egg, relish, celery, mayonnaise, lemon juice, salt, and pepper and mix thoroughly.

2. Place a leaf of lettuce on two of the slices of bread; add a slice or two of tomato, if desired; top with tuna and second bread slice. Cut in half and serve.

HELP NOTE: *The variations on this recipe are endless: capers, red onion, apple, and avocado can all be added.*

What's important is that the bread be soft (but not the type of bread you turn into spitballs).

Do not substitute fresh tuna for canned tuna!

To streamline a tuna sandwich, use water-packed tuna and light mayonnaise. You may have to add an extra tablespoon of mayo. ❦

EVEN BETTER
TUNA SANDWICH

*O*kay. This is the way I really like my tuna salad—as a coarse pâté and sort of runny. It brings back memories of the tuna fish sandwiches at Liggett's Drugstore in my hometown, Waterbury, Connecticut, in the 1940s. There are hints of sweetness from the relish, hints of onion, and only a nominal crunch from the celery. This is wonderful on good-quality soft white bread.

yield: 2 sandwiches

One 6- or 7-ounce can albacore tuna in
   oil, drained
¼ cup coarsely chopped celery
1 tablespoon coarsely chopped onion
2 tablespoons drained sweet pickle relish

4 tablespoons mayonnaise
2 teaspoons lemon juice
Salt and freshly ground black pepper
   to taste

1. Place all the ingredients in a food processor and process until the consistency of a pâté.

HELP NOTE: *Canned Italian tuna is excellent.*
   To streamline a tuna sandwich, you can use water-packed tuna and light mayonnaise, in which case you may have to add an extra tablespoon of mayonnaise. ❦

LOBSTER ROLL

A small container of very freshly cooked lobster meat caught my eye in a fish market in Vermont one day, and the first thing that popped into my head was *lobster roll!*

Now, maybe you have to have spent some time as a young child on some New England boardwalk, preferably in Maine or Massachusetts, to feel as I do about lobster rolls. And maybe you have to have been elbow-deep in steamed lobsters in your youth. But that incredibly simple combination of sweet, succulent lobster, luxuriating in mayonnaise with celery minced *so* fine you get the crunch without the taste, a touch of lemon juice on a warm, buttery bun . . . Well, maybe you have to have been there. But I *was*. Shrimp rolls and crab rolls just don't make the grade.

Think of it this way: What an inexpensive way to get the lobster thrill!

Don't buy canned or frozen lobster—it's fresh or nothing.

It's pretty amazing to drive through New England in the summer and see McDonald's offering lobster rolls. Until you taste them!

yield: 2 servings

4 ounces cooked lobster meat, cut in
  ½- to ¼-inch chunks
1 tablespoon finely minced celery
1 tablespoon lemon juice

4 to 5 tablespoons mayonnaise
Soft butter
2 top-slice hot dog rolls, split almost all the
  way through (see Help Note below)

1. Fold the lobster meat, celery, and lemon juice into the mayonnaise.

2. Butter the inside of the hot dog rolls and toast them until golden.

3. Stuff the warm rolls with the lobster mixture and serve.

HELP NOTE: *In New England the hot dog rolls used for a lobster roll do not look like hot dog rolls elsewhere in the country. Hot dog rolls from New England are sliced at the top, not the side.* 🌿

CUCUMBER ONION SALAD

$\mathcal{T}$his was one of my mother's favorite summer salads; it was, and is, almost effortless to make. I have taken liberties with it, changing the yellow onion to red, the white distilled vinegar to rice vinegar, and adding a bit of thyme. Instead of using cucumbers with thick green skins, I use Kirbys, the cucumbers my mother used for pickling.

yield: 4 servings

½ cup rice vinegar
4 teaspoons superfine sugar
4 teaspoons fresh thyme leaves

4 large Kirby cucumbers, scrubbed but
   not peeled
4 thin slices red onion, chopped

1. Stir the vinegar with the sugar and thyme.

2. Thinly slice the cucumbers and stir into the dressing with the onion. Serve immediately or allow to rest a couple of hours. 🌿

TOMATO MOZZARELLA SALAD

I hadn't thought to include this recipe until I received a phone call from a friend just as I was finishing the book, asking me what kind of vinegar to drizzle on a tomato, mozzarella, and basil salad.

No to the vinegar. Olive oil, preferably very fruity, is the drizzle of choice. And it goes without saying the tomatoes must be summer's ripest, with the perfect balance of acidity and sweetness, and the basil the most flavorful. As for the mozzarella, only the freshest will do. If you can find buffalo milk mozzarella, it has a deliciously gamy taste not found in the much blander cow's milk version. If you should be extremely lucky, you may run into a *burratta* at an Italian market. *Burratta* is mozzarella into whose center cream is poured. Think about it!

In New York you can find *burratta* at Agata & Valentina on the corner of Seventy-ninth Street and First Avenue, but call first; it is flown in only once a week and you have to be in New York to get it. I'm sure other large cities with significant Italian populations are getting it now, too.

For fresh mozzarella, see Sources, page 203.

COLESLAW

$\mathcal{S}$mall is beautiful in this old-fashioned version of coleslaw. I don't like thick strands of cabbage or carrots, and I don't like to crunch down on big pieces of onion.

yield: 6 to 8 servings

4 cups finely shredded green cabbage
1 cup finely shredded carrots
1 very small green bell pepper, finely
   shredded or chopped
2 tablespoons minced onion
1 cup mayonnaise
1 teaspoon celery seed

1½ teaspoons sugar
4 tablespoons white distilled vinegar
2 tablespoons sour cream
¼ to ½ teaspoon dry mustard
Salt and freshly ground black pepper
   to taste

1. Mix all the ingredients together and chill a few hours, or overnight, to meld the flavors.

HELP NOTE: *Use the fine shredder of the food processor to shred the cabbage, carrots, and green pepper.*

   For a streamlined version use light mayonnaise and reduced-fat sour cream. Use the larger amount of dry mustard and 3 tablespoons of white distilled vinegar. 🌾

GREEK SALAD

So this doesn't resemble the last Greek salad you had in a Greek restaurant. It certainly doesn't resemble the first Greek salad I ever had. But I discovered that there is no such thing as a definitive recipe for what we call Greek salad and the Greeks calls *horiátiki salata*.

For one thing, the dried oregano has been replaced by fresh. For another, the green pepper, not always present, has been changed to yellow pepper. The cucumber is now a Kirby and is not peeled.

And just as we can easily get fresh herbs and different color peppers, we can find real Greek olives and no longer have to rely on the ones that come from California in a can.

This version is a stunner: gorgeous colors—yellow, black, red, green, white—with intense flavors.

yield: 6 to 8 servings as a salad or 3 to 4 servings as a main course

6 tablespoons peppery extra virgin olive oil
2 tablespoons white wine vinegar
1 large yellow bell pepper, trimmed, seeded, and cut into narrow strips
2 Kirby cucumbers, unpeeled, washed, trimmed, and cut in 1/8-inch-thick round slices

2 green onions, white and light green part only, thinly sliced
20 pitted Kalamata olives, halved
2 large ripe tomatoes, cut in eighths
1 tablespoon chopped fresh oregano
4 ounces feta cheese, preferably Greek
Salt to taste

1. Whisk together the oil and vinegar; set aside.

2. In a serving bowl, combine the pepper, cucumbers, green onions, olives, and tomatoes. Sprinkle with the oregano and crumble the cheese over the mixture. Season with the salt; whisk the dressing once more, pour it over the salad, and mix well.

HELP NOTE: *Above all, pick the very best tomatoes you can find in season. Whether they are yellow or zebra-striped or white, it doesn't make any difference. Flavor is all that matters.*
Greek cooks strew all kinds of fresh herbs in season over the salad. 🌿

CHOPPED SALAD

*C*obb salad, made famous in 1926, 1936, or 1937, depending on your sources, at the equally famous Brown Derby in Los Angeles, may have been the original chopped salad. The perfect chopped salad is a balance of sweet, sour, salty, and bitter and should take advantage of seasonal ingredients.

yield: 10 generous servings

1 large head romaine lettuce

1 large bunch arugula

1 pound ripe tomatoes, washed, stemmed, and cut into bite-size wedges

2 medium yellow bell peppers, washed, trimmed, seeded, and cut into 1/4-Inch dice

2 medium avocados, cut into 1/4-inch dice

3/4 cup minced red onion

2/3 cup olives, such as Cerignola or Kalamata, pitted and quartered

3 hard-cooked eggs

DRESSING

3/4 cup extra virgin olive oil

3 tablespoons white wine vinegar

1 tablespoon Dijon mustard

Salt and freshly ground black pepper to taste

1. Slice off the crunchy white from the bottom of the romaine; discard. Wash and dry the green part and roughly chop or break up into bite-size pieces.

2. Remove the tough stems from the arugula; discard; wash, dry, and roughly tear leaves into bite-size pieces.

3. Place all the ingredients but the eggs in a salad bowl.

4. Whisk the Dressing ingredients together and toss with the salad at least 15 minutes before serving so that the ingredients can absorb it.

5. Sieve the eggs and sprinkle them over the salad.

HELP NOTE: *The main ingredient in a chopped salad is lettuce, but it can contain anything you want. The most important rule for this salad is that the ingredients are cut in pieces that are still recognizable but blend well with the other ingredients. It must have a dressing that is thick enough so that everything clings together. To make the salad a little more substantial you can add 1/2 cup crumbled feta, goat, or blue cheese.*

Unlike most salads, which should be dressed at the last minute, this is one in which the dressing should be mixed with the ingredients 15 minutes before serving to blend the flavors. ✿

CAESAR SALAD

The popularity of Caesar salad has waxed and waned ever since it was created in Tijuana, Mexico, in the 1920s. It is currently at the top of its game, anointed with everything from chicken to shrimp, turning it into a main-dish salad.

But I like mine the way I first had it—with everything mixed together, the croutons toasted lightly, and slightly soft so that they don't cut the inside of your mouth. They should be flavored not only with garlic but with a fruity olive oil.

It took me a while to figure out the crucial difference between the new Caesar salads and the ones I used to love: the quantity of the dressing. As you will see, there is no stinting here.

yield: 6 servings

4 tablespoons PLUS ¾ cup extra virgin olive oil

6 medium cloves garlic, crushed

2 cups diced high-quality white bread, such as a baguette

12 cups washed and dried romaine leaves, broken into pieces, green part only

2 tablespoons lemon juice

1 tablespoon Worcestershire sauce

8 or more flat anchovy fillets, mashed

3 eggs, boiled medium soft

Salt and freshly ground black pepper to taste

¾ cup freshly grated Parmigiano-Reggiano (see Sources, page 203)

1. Heat 4 tablespoons oil in a sauté pan. Add the garlic and diced bread and sauté over medium heat, stirring often until the croutons are lightly browned and crisp. Discard the garlic. Place the croutons on a paper towel.

2. Place romaine in a large salad bowl.

3. Whisk the lemon juice and Worcestershire sauce into the remaining ¾ cup oil. Mix in the anchovies.

4. Coarsely chop the eggs and add to the romaine.

5. Pour the dressing over the lettuce and mix well to coat each leaf. Season with salt and pepper. Stir in the croutons. Sprinkle with the Parmigiano-Reggiano and toss again.

HELP NOTE: *Most people these days would rather not eat raw or coddled eggs. You can buy pasteurized eggs, but I prefer to boil the eggs until they are cooked medium with a soft but formed yolk and white. Place the eggs in gently boiling water; cover the pan, remove from the heat, and let the eggs stand 5 minutes.*

TARRAGON VINAIGRETTE

I like this spooned over steamed asparagus or shrimp, or mixed with chicken salad.

yield: about ¾ cup

1 tablespoon red wine vinegar
1 tablespoon tarragon vinegar
½ cup extra virgin olive oil
2 teaspoons or more Dijon mustard

1 tablespoon chopped fresh tarragon
1 tablespoon chopped fresh parsley
Salt and freshly ground black pepper
  to taste

1. Whisk together the vinegars, oil, and mustard until emulsified. Stir in the remaining ingredients.

VARIATIONS: You can use any other herb in the same proportion: thyme, oregano, basil, or rosemary. Omit the tarragon vinegar and add another tablespoon of red wine vinegar. If you use basil, do not stir it in until the last minute; fresh basil turns an unattractive black color and wilts.

HELP NOTE: The dressing can be made a day ahead, refrigerated covered, and whisked just before using. 🌿

BLUE CHEESE DRESSING

At one point, everything that didn't have French dressing on it was covered with blue cheese dressing. This is my favorite version: tangy, not too thick, and with an interesting crunch from the walnuts.

yield: 6 to 8 servings for a salad of romaine or, if you must, iceberg lettuce

½ cup mayonnaise
½ cup sour cream
¼ cup milk
¼ teaspoon minced garlic
2 teaspoons red wine vinegar

6 to 8 tablespoons crumbled blue cheese
Couple shakes cayenne pepper
Freshly ground black pepper to taste
Heaping ¼ cup coarsely chopped toasted
  walnuts

1. Whisk together the mayonnaise, sour cream, and milk until well blended. Stir in the garlic and vinegar.

2. Add the blue cheese and stir well to mix thoroughly. Season with the cayenne and pepper and stir in the walnuts.

HELP NOTE: *For a streamlined version: With all the strong flavors in this dressing, you can comfortably substitute light mayonnaise, low-fat sour cream, and low-fat or skim milk for their full-fat counterparts. Use only 6 tablespoons of the blue cheese. It's almost impossible to tell which is the low-fat and which is the full-fat version. Depending on how intense you want the blue cheese flavor, you can use the so-called sweet Gorgonzola, which is much gentler than regular Gorgonzola. Bleu de Bresse and Maytag Blue are similar to Gorgonzola, as is Roquefort. Stilton is milder than Roquefort.* 🌿

GREEN GODDESS DRESSING

*G*reen Goddess Dressing was created at the Palace Hotel in San Francisco to honor a hit play of the 1920s, *The Green Goddess*. It was written by William Archer and starred the great English actor George Arliss.

At some point there must have been the one, the only, the original, but now you'd be hard-pressed to tell from all the variations in today's cookbooks. The green in this recipe appears as flecks in the creamy white dressing.

Serve this over romaine lettuce or as a dressing for seafood salads.

yield: 1 cup

½ cup mayonnaise
½ cup sour cream
1 tablespoon tarragon vinegar
¼ cup chopped fresh parsley

8 flat anchovy fillets
4 tablespoons chopped chives or
    green onions

1. Place all the ingredients in a food processor or blender and process until well blended.

HELP NOTE: The dressing can be made on the morning of the day it is to be used.

If you are a tarragon fan you can add a little fresh tarragon, but go easy: tarragon is a powerful herb.

To make a streamlined Green Goddess, substitute light mayonnaise and reduced-fat sour cream. Only if you taste them side by side can you tell the difference between the streamlined and the traditional versions. ❧

MEAT

BOB JAMIESON'S ORIGINAL MEAT LOAF

*B*ob was uncomplaining when I turned his meat loaf into a lower-fat dish many years ago. I think it is delicious that way, but Bob doesn't like it with other "stuff" in it. In tribute to the best meat loaf I ever ate, full fat or otherwise, here's the original version he gave me twenty years ago.

Bob, a correspondent for ABC News, says "It's ideal with baked potatoes and canned peas." (I prefer to use frozen.)

yield: 8 slices

1 tablespoon unsalted butter	2 lightly beaten eggs
1 large onion, finely chopped	2 tablespoons Dijon mustard
1½ pounds ground beef, room temperature	¼ cup catsup, PLUS 5 tablespoons for glazing
1½ pounds ground veal, room temperature	3 tablespoons saltine cracker crumbs
1½ pounds ground pork, room temperature	Salt and freshly ground black pepper to taste
3 tablespoons Worcestershire sauce	2 strips bacon, optional

1. Set a rack in the middle of the oven. Preheat the oven to 350 degrees.

2. Melt the butter; sauté the onion in the butter over medium heat until it is quite soft and golden. Add to the meats along with the Worcestershire, eggs, mustard, ¼ cup catsup, cracker crumbs, and salt and pepper. Using your hands, gently mix the ingredients until well blended.

3. Spoon the mixture into a 9 by 5-inch loaf pan and pat gently. Spread the remaining catsup over the top and lay the bacon slices over the loaf, if desired.

4. Bake for 50 to 60 minutes. Remove from the oven and drain off the fat. Allow the loaf to sit for 5 minutes and slice and serve.

WINE: *Shiraz, Côtes du Rhône, or Sangiovese*

HELP NOTE: *Grind the beef yourself. The meat loaf can be made ahead and refrigerated, covered. To serve, allow to sit at room temperature and then bake according to directions.*

The meat loaf is good cold in a sandwich, of course, but the only way you'll have leftovers is if you serve it to four people instead of eight.

The catsup of choice is Heinz.

JIM BRADY'S PRIZE-WINNING GOAT GAP CHILI

I first met Jim Brady when he was the newly minted press secretary for President Ronald Reagan. He loved to eat and he loved to cook, and I spent an afternoon at his house while he made chili. Not long after I wrote about that afternoon for *The Washington Post*, Jim was shot by John Hinckley, Jr., and permanently disabled. A bullet meant for President Reagan hit Brady instead.

Even twenty years after Jim's injury he continues to improve. Every time we visit we have some conversation about food.

He and his wife, Sarah, generously agreed to let me use the chili recipe for which he is now famous.

Serve with Jalapeño Corn Bread Pudding (page 137).

yield: 8 servings

6 tablespoons oil

2 pounds round steak, cut in cubes

1 pound pork tenderloin, cut in cubes

2 tablespoons pure hot chile powder, more or less (depending on heat desired)

3 medium onions, chopped

3 large jalapeños, more or less, seeded and minced

4 cloves garlic, minced

1 tablespoon dried oregano

1 tablespoon red wine vinegar

One 28-ounce can crushed tomatoes

1 cup water

3 bay leaves

4 teaspoons ground cumin

1 tablespoon brown sugar

1 teaspoon salt

One 6-ounce can pitted California olives, optional

Shredded aged Cheddar for garnish

1. Heat 3 tablespoons of oil in a large pot and brown the beef and the pork in the fat. Stir in the chili powder and set aside.

2. Heat the remaining oil in a large skillet and sauté the onions until golden.

3. Add the jalapeños and sauté for a minute or two; add the garlic and sauté for 30 seconds.

4. Add the onion mixture to the meat along with the oregano, vinegar, tomatoes, water, bay leaves, cumin, brown sugar, salt, and olives, if desired. Reduce the heat to a low simmer.

5. Cover and cook for 2½ hours; do not boil. Stir occasionally and adjust the seasoning if needed.

6. Remove and discard the bay leaves and top with Cheddar before serving.

WINE: *Sangiovese, Zinfandel; for the spicier versions Riesling, Gewürztraminer, or beer*

HELP NOTE: *You can make this dish much hotter; Jim always did. His version calls for four jalapeños and a 2.4-ounce box of pure hot chile powder!*

This can be made ahead and refrigerated for up to 3 days. It can be frozen for a month but adjust the seasonings before serving.

Be sure to test the japaleños before using them: some are hot, some are very mild. ❦

BEEF STEW IN WINE

I tried this stew with beer, but it has none of the depth of flavor and richness that it has when made with an intense red wine.

yield: 12 servings

4 pounds chuck or bottom rump, trimmed of fat and cut in 1½-inch cubes

Salt and freshly ground black pepper to taste

½ cup flour PLUS ⅓ cup, optional

4 tablespoons oil

2 pounds carrots, finely chopped, PLUS 1 pound carrots, cut in 1-inch chunks, or peeled whole baby carrots

2 pounds onions, coarsely chopped

4 large cloves garlic, sliced

4 cups red wine, such as Cabernet Sauvignon

4 cups good-quality beef stock

2 to 3 tablespoons each fresh oregano and fresh thyme, or 2 to 3 teaspoons each dried oregano and dried thyme

2 bay leaves

2 pounds new potatoes, unpeeled, cut in 1-inch chunks

1½ to 2 pounds rutabagas, peeled and cut in ½-inch chunks

1. Season the beef cubes with the salt and pepper. Roll in the ½ cup flour.

2. Heat the oil to high in a nonstick pan large enough to hold the beef in a single layer. (Most people won't have this size pan, so use two pans; even my 16-inch pan was too small.)

3. Brown the beef cubes on all sides; set aside. Add the 2 pounds finely chopped carrots and cook over high heat until they begin to brown. Add the onions and cook over medium-high heat until the onions are soft and golden. The carrots should be well browned. If necessary, add more oil. Add the garlic and sauté 30 seconds.

4. Return the beef to the pan with the vegetables and add the wine, stock, oregano, thyme, and bay leaves. Bring to a boil and reduce the heat to a simmer. Cover and cook for about 1 hour. The beef will still be slightly tough.

5. Add the remaining 1 pound carrots, potatoes, and rutabagas and continue cooking about an hour longer, until the vegetables and meat are tender. Adjust the seasoning, remove and discard the bay leaves, and serve.

WINE *Cabernet Sauvignon, Spanish Ribera, or French Bordeaux*

HELP NOTE: *For a thicker stew, whisk ⅓ cup flour with ⅓ cup cool water, making sure there are no lumps. Just before serving, add this mixture to the stew, a little at a time, stirring, until the gravy is the thickness you desire. Heat well.*

The onions and carrots can be chopped in a food processor.

Browning some of the carrots before stewing adds sweetness and richness and makes a big difference in the final dish.

This dish is really best the second day, after it has chilled, the fat has been skimmed from the top, and the flavors have had a chance to meld. Reheat slowly.

The recipe is large because the stew freezes beautifully for up to a month.

If you want to mash the vegetables in the sauce, cook them longer; if you like them in the contemporary fashion, tender but still firm, cook them less.

The rump is leaner and, therefore, not as juicy or fatty as the chuck. ❦

MY MOTHER'S "MODERN" BRISKET

$\mathcal{T}$his was one of my mother's standbys. She made it without the tomatoey sauce; I added that later.

yield: 12 servings

3 pounds onions, chopped
3 tablespoons oil
One 6-pound first-cut brisket, external fat
   removed
Salt

1 cup catsup
5 to 6 tablespoons lemon juice or more
2 tablespoons packed dark brown sugar
2 cups canned tomato puree

1. Using a large pan so the onions can be spread out, sauté the onions in the hot oil until they are golden.

2. Over high heat brown the brisket well on both sides in its own fat in a large, heavy-bottomed pot. Season with salt and add the onions. Cover and cook over very low heat so that the fat and juices from the meat just simmer. Turn a couple of times and cook 3 to 4 hours, until fork-tender.

3. This step is not essential but I like to do it: Pour off the juices and put them in a pan in the freezer. Check after about an hour and you should be able to skim off the fat. If necessary, allow the juices to rest longer but don't let them freeze.

4. Return the defatted juices to the brisket with the catsup, lemon juice, brown sugar, and tomato puree, and cook for another 30 minutes. Remove the brisket from the pot, slice it thinly across the grain, and return the meat to the sauce to keep warm.

MY MOTHER'S ORIGINAL VERSION: *Follow the recipe above but do not add the catsup, lemon juice, brown sugar, or tomato puree. Brisket makes its own gravy, so the tomato sauce mixture is not essential, just tasty.*

   My mother always served her brisket with a mixture of bow tie noodles, buckwheat groats, and onions sautéed in chicken fat.

WINE: *For the version with sauce serve Gewürztraminer; for my mother's version, light Zinfandel, Shiraz, or Sangiovese.*

HELP NOTE: *Because brisket has so much fat, it shrinks considerably during the cooking process.*

The brisket and its sauce can be refrigerated or frozen before the final cooking in step 4 for up to a month. Defrost if frozen and reheat slowly. This dish improves when reheated. ❦

BRAISED SHORT RIBS

*T*he reason the ribs are so succulent, of course, is that they are so well marbled, but every once in a while, what a way to get warm.

yield: 4 servings

4 pounds beef short ribs, each 2 inches
   square, or flanken short ribs
Salt and freshly ground black pepper
   to taste
I tablespoon olive oil
I large onion, coarsely chopped
I carrot, peeled and coarsely chopped
I leek, white part only, trimmed and
   coarsely chopped

3 cloves garlic, smashed
3 sprigs thyme
I large sprig rosemary
I bay leaf
2 cups canned plum tomatoes, without
   juice from can
¾ cup dry red wine
2 cups good-quality hot beef stock

1. Place a rack in the lower third of the oven. Preheat the oven to 475 degrees.

2. Season the ribs with salt and pepper. Arrange bone side down in a roasting pan and roast for 20 minutes. Remove from the pan and set aside. Wipe out the fat from the pan. Reduce the heat to 350 degrees.

3. In a skillet heat the oil and sauté the onion over medium-high heat until it takes on color. Add the carrot and leek and continue sautéing over medium heat until the vegetables begin to soften.

4. Add the garlic, thyme, rosemary, bay leaf, and plum tomatoes, crushed in your hand before adding. Cook another couple of minutes over medium heat.

5. Add the wine and cook a couple of minutes more at medium-high heat until reduced just a little. Spread the vegetable mixture over the bottom of the roasting pan. Place the ribs on top of the vegetables, bone side up. Add the hot beef stock, cover the pan with foil, and bring to a boil on top of the stove.

6. Loosen the foil and place the pan in the oven. Braise for about 1½ hours. Ribs are done when the meat is falling off the bone. Test with a knife.

7. Drain the liquid from the pan and reserve. Turn the oven to 450 degrees. Turn the ribs bone side down and return to the oven for about 10 minutes until they are dark brown.

8. Strain the vegetables, remove the bay leaf, and press on the vegetables to extract all their flavor into the liquid. Allow to sit so that the fat rises to the top. Skim off the fat and serve the ribs in the strained liquid.

WINE: *hearty Cabernet Sauvignon, Bordeaux*

HELP NOTE: *If the ribs are not being served immediately, refrigerate them and the juices separately. The fat will harden and will be easier to remove. To serve, slowly reheat the ribs in the juices in a covered pot on top of the stove.*

This is delicious with noodles, Mashed Potatoes (see page 130), or baked potatoes and turnips or rutabagas. 🌿

HUNGARIAN GOULASH

*Y*es, yes. I know this is not authentic Hungarian goulash or *gulyas*. It should not have sour cream; it should not have sauerkraut, etc., etc. So if you want to call it something else, please do. But do try to get sweet Hungarian paprika, because it is quite flavorful, unlike the paprika we find in the supermarket.

The paprika, by the way, did not become part of the *gulyas* until the eighteenth century, though the original recipe dates back to ninth-century Magyar shepherds.

yield: 6 servings

3 large onions, finely chopped
8 slices reduced-fat nitrite-free bacon, coarsely diced
3 tablespoons olive oil
3 large cloves garlic, minced
1 medium green bell pepper, julienned
1 medium red bell pepper, julienned
3 tablespoons sweet Hungarian paprika
2 pounds lean boneless pork, such as tenderloin, cut in ¾-inch cubes

Salt and freshly ground black pepper to taste
2 teaspoons caraway seed
2 cups water
2 pounds fresh sauerkraut
¾ pound highly seasoned sausage
6 ounces sour cream
1 pound egg noodles, cooked

The day before you plan to serve the goulash:

1. In a large pot, sauté the onions and bacon in hot oil until the onions begin to soften. Add the garlic and peppers and continue cooking until the vegetables are soft.

2. Remove from the heat and stir in the paprika; mix well. Add the pork cubes and stir to coat. Cook over low heat for a few minutes to color the pork. Season with salt, pepper, and caraway seed.

3. Add water, cover the pot, and simmer 45 minutes.

4. Wash the sauerkraut under cold running water and squeeze dry. Add the sauerkraut and the sausage to the meat and cook another 15 minutes. Meat should be very tender.

5. Refrigerate the goulash, covered, so the flavors can meld.

6. To serve, reheat thoroughly. Reduce the heat to simmer, and stir in the sour cream; adjust seasonings. Serve over the egg noodles.

WINE: *Shiraz, Syrah, Côtes du Rhône, or an intense Zinfandel*

HELP NOTE: *If Hungarian paprika is not available locally, see Sources, page 203. See Sources, page 204, for nitrite-free bacon.* ❦

SLOPPY JOES

*P*urported to have made their first appearance in the 1950s, these hot sandwiches appeal because they take no time to make at all and are a combination of what most of us love best—spaghetti sauce and barbecue sauce. You are likely to have most, if not all, the ingredients in the house.

I have made several changes to bring up the flavor, and I suspect your kids will love them.

yield: 4 servings

1 tablespoon olive oil
1 large onion, finely chopped
½ cup finely chopped celery
½ large green bell pepper, finely chopped
1 large clove garlic, minced
1½ pounds ground beef or bison
1 cup beer
¼ cup Worcestershire sauce

½ cup catsup
2 teaspoons Dijon mustard
4 teaspoons white vinegar
¼ to 1 teaspoon hot pepper sauce
Salt and freshly ground black pepper
  to taste
Toasted rolls, such as hamburger buns

1. Heat the oil; sauté the onion in the hot oil for about 3 minutes. Add the celery and green pepper and continue sautéing until the vegetables are soft and taking on color.

2. Add the garlic and sauté for 30 seconds. Push the vegetables to the side and add the beef, breaking it up with a fork until meat is crumbled. Cook until the meat is cooked through and no pink remains.

3. Add the beer, Worcestershire, catsup, mustard, vinegar, and hot pepper sauce, reduce the heat, and simmer a few minutes until the flavors are blended. Season with the salt and pepper.

4. Serve on rolls as open or closed sandwiches.

WINE: *Just beer*

HELP NOTE: *I use ground bison or I grind my own beef. I don't buy ground beef because I have no idea how healthy the animals were from which it came. If you can't find ground bison locally, you can order it on the Web (see Sources, page 204).*

Sloppy Joes are just as good, maybe better, the second day. They can also be frozen for up to a month. To serve, simply reheat. ❦

BARBECUED SPARERIBS

*M*y significant other, Roy, loved the ribs our friends Beverly and John Sullivan served us at their house in Rappahannock County, Virginia, so much he asked for the recipe. John seemed reluctant to share, a smile playing around his lips. Finally he confessed his secret ingredient—Lowry's Seasoning Salt.

I wasn't about to use that, if for no other reason than the fact that the amount of salt in it makes my mouth go dry. I don't have to save money by substituting salt for seasoning, so I created my own rub and after a couple of tries have come up with one that Roy likes so well, he wants ribs for dinner at least once a week.

yield: 4 to 6 servings

2 tablespoons paprika
1 teaspoon coarsely ground black pepper
1 teaspoon lemon pepper
2 teaspoons garlic powder
2 teaspoons onion powder
2 teaspoons brown sugar

1 teaspoon dry mustard
1 teaspoon salt
¼ teaspoon cayenne pepper, or more
   to taste
5 pounds baby back spareribs

1. Combine all the ingredients but the pork for the rub.

2. If you wish, remove the papery skin from the back of each rack by pulling it off with your fingers, or just slit it with a knife.

3. Spread the rub generously on both sides of the ribs. Allow the ribs to sit in the refrigerator for up to 8 hours or at room temperature for 1 hour. For the fire, use charcoal and wood chips.

4. Cook over direct heat until the ribs are browned. Lower the fire and place the charcoal and wood to each side. Place a large drip pan under the ribs in the center. Continue cooking the ribs over indirect heat until the ribs are done. How long depends on your grill, your fire, distance from fire, etc. To test, cut into the ribs in the middle: The meat should not be pink. Use vents to regulate the heat.

WINE: *Côtes du Rhône, Shiraz, or Syrah*

HELP NOTE: *Baby backs are the best, meatier and less fatty than other varieties.*
   I've taken off the papery skin from the backs of the racks and I have left it on. I have a pretty hard time telling the difference. The seasoning makes its way to the ribs either way.

(continued)

Ribs are tricky: Sometimes they are done in an hour, sometimes 1½ hours.

This rub is delicious on grilled chicken, too.

I can't remember the last time I used onion powder or garlic powder or lemon pepper, if I ever used that at all, but they are a must for a dry rub.

I prefer a dry rub to a sauce. It has just as much flavor, and you can always add sauce at the table if you like. But these ribs don't need it.

The best charcoal is actually charwood. It's better for the environment and makes a great hot fire. People's Woods in Rhode Island sells charwood, wood, and wood chips. See Sources, page 204. 🌿

GRILLED BUTTERFLIED
LEG OF LAMB

The memories of leg of lamb from my childhood conjure up mystery meat with mint jelly at Sunday dinner at school. It took me years to get over my dislike of lamb.

yield: 6 to 8 servings

One 4-pound leg of lamb, boned and
    butterflied
1 bottle good-quality dry red wine
1 ½ cups olive oil
1 tablespoon Dijon mustard
3 very large cloves garlic or 6 medium
    cloves, coarsely chopped

3 medium onions, cut in eighths
6 to 8 branches thyme
6 thin branches rosemary
Salt and freshly ground black pepper
    to taste

1. Wash and dry the lamb; remove all the excess fat and sinews.

2. Combine the remaining ingredients in a bowl large enough to hold the lamb. Place the lamb in the bowl, making sure most of the lamb is covered with the liquid. Cover and marinate the lamb in the refrigerator for at least 2 hours, or ideally, overnight.

3. To serve, heat the grill until it is very hot and brush the grill with oil. Drain the lamb, reserve the marinade, and sear the meat over the high heat, about 2 minutes on each side.

4. Lower the heat or raise the grill higher above the heat, or move the charcoal to the sides. Grill another 5 to 8 minutes, depending on how rare you want the meat. Remove the lamb to a platter, cover, and let the meat reabsorb its juices, about 10 minutes.

5. Meanwhile, boil the marinade to reduce by about half. Strain into a small pot. Pour the juices that have not been absorbed into the pot and heat through. Adjust the seasonings; slice the lamb and serve with the pan juices. The meat is best served rare, sliced thinly.

WINE: *Shiraz Cabernet or a Shiraz*

(continued)

HELP NOTE: *You can use any combination of herbs you prefer, but rosemary and lamb are a natural. This marinade does not overwhelm the taste of the lamb; it enhances it and tenderizes it.*

This is an easy and impressive meal for the outdoor chef to make, but I've done it very successfully on the top of the stove on a stove-top grill.

My housekeeper, Elsa Castro, looked at the onions in the marinade and said, "You must cook them and serve them with the lamb." So I did, for about 10 minutes, with some of the marinade in a pot. Then the mixture was placed in a sauté pan and the onions were sautéed until they were very tender. Elsa was right; they were superb with the lamb.

Use the same wine for the marinade and for drinking. ❦

POULTRY

GREAT ROAST CHICKEN

*T*his is the way chicken is roasted at Bouley restaurant in New York City. It calls for the very best chicken you can find, and that is likely to be an organic bird. The steaming and vertical roasting are the keys to great flavor.

yield: 2 servings

One 3- to 3½-pound organic chicken (see Sources, page 204)
1 sprig thyme
1 sprig rosemary
1 sprig sage

2 large cloves garlic, halved
1 lemon, halved
Salt and freshly ground black pepper
Hungarian sweet paprika

1. Set a rack in the lower third of the oven. Preheat the oven to 375 degrees. Boil enough water to fill a roasting pan halfway up.

2. Wash and dry the chicken. Remove the first two joints of the wings, and discard. Stuff the inside of the chicken with thyme, rosemary, sage, and two garlic halves.

3. Rub the lemon, salt, and pepper all over the chicken. Rub with the remaining garlic and sprinkle heavily with paprika to coat completely. Place the chicken on a rack set on top of the roasting pan and steam over boiling water in the oven for 20 minutes. Remove from the oven and place the chicken on a vertical roaster, following the manufacturer's directions for positioning. Pour off the water and place the chicken in the pan.

4. Reduce the oven to 350 degrees, and roast the chicken about 20 minutes longer, until juices from the breast run clear when cut with a knife. Remove from the vertical roaster and cut off the legs at the joint where the thigh meets the body. Return the legs to the pan and roast about 10 minutes longer, until the juices run clear.

5. Allow the chicken to rest 10 minutes and then remove the herbs from the cavity. Remove skin. Cut off each breast in one piece and slice ¼ inch thick on a diagonal. To serve the legs, remove the skin, remove meat from the bone, and cut into bite-size pieces.

WINE: *Burgundy or Côtes du Rhône, Pinot Noir, Shiraz, or Cabernet Sauvignon*

HELP NOTE: *You will need to buy a small, inexpensive vertical roaster for this recipe. They are available at most kitchenware shops or on-line. See Sources, page 204.*

CHICKEN CACCIATORE

When I finally realized I didn't have to use a whole chicken for this recipe but could pick and choose meaty pieces, Chicken Cacciatore became a staple in my house. I serve it with spaghetti.

yield: 4 or 5 servings

1 pound onions, thinly sliced (about 3 cups)

3 tablespoons olive oil or more

4 cloves garlic, minced

4 pounds chicken thighs and breasts, skinless, bone-in

½ cup dry white wine

3 pounds ripe well-flavored tomatoes, coarsely chopped, or 3 cups canned tomatoes, broken up

¼ cup tomato paste

1 teaspoon dried rosemary

¼ to ½ teaspoon hot red pepper flakes

Salt and freshly ground black pepper to taste

1. Sauté the onions in hot oil over medium-high heat until they are golden. Add the garlic and sauté another 30 seconds. Remove the onions and garlic from the pan and set aside.

2. Wash and dry the chicken and cut the chicken breasts into quarters. Place the chicken in the pan meaty side down and brown over medium-high heat. Turn and brown on second side, adding more oil if needed, topping with the browned onions and garlic.

3. Add the wine and simmer until it is reduced by half. Add the tomatoes, tomato paste, rosemary, and hot pepper flakes. Season with the salt and pepper.

4. Reduce the heat to very low; cover partially, and simmer until the chicken is very tender and comes away easily from bone, about 30 minutes. Turn the chicken occasionally. If the sauce becomes too thick, add a little water.

WINE: *Sangiovese or light Zinfandel, Chardonnay, or Sauvignon Blanc*

HELP NOTE: *This dish can be prepared a day ahead and reheated slowly. (It is actually better prepared a day ahead.) It can be frozen, too, if well wrapped, for up to a month.*

It's great accompanied by very garlicky Garlic Bread (page 136).

If your tomatoes are not very flavorful, add an additional 2 to 4 tablespoons of tomato paste. If using canned tomatoes, the best are San Marzano. They are now turning up in supermarkets and are certainly available in Italian markets or on the Web (see Sources, page 204).

CHICKEN POTPIE WITH PHYLLO CRUST

*M*ost of the chicken potpie fillings I have eaten in my life have reminded me of chicken à la king: pale, gluey, and tasteless with bits of pimiento floating around in it. So I wasn't inclined to include potpie until my friend Joan Hamburg, who has a very popular call-in show on WOR radio in New York, said everyone in New York is eating chicken potpies because they are comfort food. "Even the rail-thin women," she said.

Making chicken potpies is an undertaking, but using phyllo dough for a crust cuts down the work significantly.

yield: 4 to 6 servings

1 heaping cup pearl onions	2 tablespoons oil
1 ½ pounds skinless chicken breasts	½ pound shiitake mushrooms, washed,
1 ½ pounds skinless chicken thighs	stemmed, and cut in ¼-inch strips
20 baby carrots, peeled	1 cup fresh or frozen peas
1 leek, white part only, trimmed and sliced	2 tablespoons lemon juice
4 sprigs thyme, PLUS 2 tablespoons	8 tablespoons (1 stick) unsalted butter
chopped fresh thyme	½ cup flour
Salt and freshly ground black pepper	2 cups reserved chicken stock
to taste	1 cup heavy cream
1 large red bell pepper	¼ to ½ teaspoon ground nutmeg
1 large yellow bell pepper	Phyllo Topping (see recipe, page 98)

1. Plunge the pearl onions in boiling water for 30 seconds and drain. Cut off the root end and slip the outside skin off the onions. Set aside.

2. Cut each whole chicken breast into quarters. In a pot, combine the chicken breasts and thighs, onions, carrots, leek, and 4 sprigs of thyme. Season with the salt and pepper. Add water just to cover. Cover the pot and bring to a boil. Reduce the heat and simmer for about 20 minutes, until the chicken is cooked.

3. Meanwhile trim, seed, and halve the peppers. Cut each half into thin strips, then cut the strips in half. Heat the oil; sauté the peppers over medium-high heat until they soften. Stir in the mushrooms and sauté until they soften, about four minutes. Set aside.

(continued)

4. When the chicken is cooked, strain, reserving the liquid. Let the chicken cool, remove the meat from the bone, and cut the meat into 1-inch chunks. Add the chicken meat to the peppers and mushrooms. Add the pearl onions. Cut twelve of the carrots in half and add. Stir in the peas, lemon juice, and chopped thyme. Discard the leek, thyme sprigs, and the remaining carrots (or use for something else).

5. Melt 8 tablespoons butter over medium heat, remove from the heat, and stir in the flour. Return to medium heat and cook, stirring, a couple of minutes until blended and bubbling. Remove from the heat and stir in the stock. Return to the heat and cook, stirring until the mixture thickens. Take the pan from the heat, cool slightly, and stir in the cream. Season with salt, pepper, and the nutmeg and stir into the chicken and vegetables. Adjust the seasonings.

PHYLLO TOPPING

> 8 phyllo leaves (see Help Note, page 99)
> 4 tablespoons melted butter for brushing

1. Place a rack in the lower third of the oven. Preheat the oven to 425 degrees.

2. Open the package of phyllo and cover with a damp towel.

3. Place a stack of 8 phyllo leaves on a work surface. Trace the top of a deep 10-inch baking dish on the pile of phyllo leaves. Cut the phyllo to fit and then cover them again. Wrap the remaining phyllo in an airtight bag and use on another occasion. Phyllo will last about a week.

4. Spoon the chicken and vegetables into the baking dish.

5. Remove one leaf, brush it with some of the melted butter, and place it butter side up on top of the chicken and vegetables in the baking dish. Butter the next leaf and place it on top of the first. Repeat until all the leaves are used and brush butter on top of the final leaf. Tuck the edges of the phyllo into the dish. Cut a 1-inch hole in the middle of the phyllo to allow steam to escape.

6. Bake for 25 to 30 minutes, until the filling is bubbly and the top is golden brown.

WINE: *light red such as Cabernet Franc, light Zinfandel, or Sangiovese*

HELP NOTE: *The filling can be made in advance and stored in the refrigerator, well covered. It must be returned to room temperature before it is baked.*

Phyllo are the paper-thin sheets of pastry used for so many Greek pastries like baklava. Many supermarkets carry them in the frozen-food section. Fresh is better, but not so easily available, unless there is a Greek market near you. Completely defrost the phyllo in the refrigerator or at room temperature before using.

If you want a thicker sauce for the filling, use an additional 2 tablespoons of flour. ❦

LIZ HAUPERT'S FRIED CHICKEN

I learned to fry chicken from Liz, my best friend in college. She was born and raised in Arkansas, and still lives there.

Liz didn't soak her chicken and she never insisted on a cast-iron skillet, but she did say that bacon grease was essential. In the days when I thought bacon grease was something to treasure and save in a coffee can, I fried some pretty good chicken for a New England native.

Oil has replaced bacon fat in this recipe, but otherwise nothing has changed. Now I buy parts instead of a whole chicken. I prefer the legs and thighs because they are juicier. The chicken still passes the test of Southern friends.

yield: 4 servings

3 to 3½ pounds chicken breasts and thighs, cut in equal-size pieces
1 to 1½ cups flour

Salt and freshly ground black pepper to taste
Corn oil for frying (about 1 quart)

1. Wash the chicken pieces and drain but do not dry.

2. Place the flour, salt, and pepper in a plastic bag and shake to mix. Add a few pieces of chicken at a time and shake to coat pieces thoroughly all over with flour. Place the coated pieces on wax paper and repeat until all the chicken is floured. Add more flour if necessary.

3. Heat enough oil in a deep, heavy skillet to cover the chicken pieces almost entirely, until the oil begins to ripple. The skillet should be large enough to accommodate all the chicken pieces in a single layer.

4. Place the chicken pieces in the hot oil skin side down and cook over high heat 10 minutes or until golden. Turn and cook 10 minutes more or until the other side is golden. The chicken should be done at this point. Cut into the thick part of a breast piece to check for doneness. If the chicken is not cooked, reduce the heat, turn the chicken, and cook a few minutes longer.

5. Remove the pieces to several layers of paper towels, drain quickly, and then place on a rack.

6. The chicken should be served warm, not hot.

WINE: *Chardonnay or Sauvignon Blanc, or Côtes du Rhône, light Pinot Noir*

HELP NOTE: *If some chicken pieces are browning more quickly than others, turn the pan around; if it is all browning too quickly, turn the heat down.*

The chicken can be held for two hours at room temperature, loosely covered with foil.

Fried chicken that has seen the inside of a refrigerator is not fried chicken anymore. ❦

PICNIC FRIED CHICKEN

Lindy Boggs, former congresswoman and ambassador to the Vatican, is a great lady and a great cook. Lindy is the one who introduced me thirty years ago to chicken fried in the oven. Over time the recipe has been refined slightly, but the biggest change is the availability of fresh Parmigiano-Reggiano instead of that grated canned stuff that passed for Parmesan cheese. What a difference!

yield: 6 to 7 servings

3 tablespoons chopped pecans
1 cup finely grated Parmigiano-Reggiano
2 cups fine dried bread crumbs
1 teaspoon each dried thyme, oregano, and basil

Salt and freshly ground black pepper to taste
Olive oil and olive oil pan spray
5 pounds skinless chicken thighs and breasts

1. Place a rack in the lower third of the oven. Preheat the oven to 400 degrees.

2. Grind the pecans finely in a food processor.

3. Process the Parmigiano-Reggiano until it is finely ground; combine with the pecans, bread crumbs, herbs, salt, and pepper.

4. Brush or spray two baking sheets with oil. Place some of the bread crumb mixture in a plastic bag.

5. Wash the chicken and cut the whole breasts into quarters. Dip each piece in water and shake a few pieces at a time in the bag until the pieces are well coated with the crumb mixture. Place the chicken meaty side down on baking sheets. Press the coating on any spots to which it does not adhere well. Repeat. Spray the bottom of chicken pieces with oil and bake for about 20 minutes, until browned on the underside. Turn and brush again with oil if the pieces seem dry. Continue baking until the chicken is cooked through and both sides are browned, about another 15 to 20 minutes.

6. Serve immediately, warm or at room temperature.

WINE: *light Pinot Noir, Sangiovese, or Chardonnay*

HELP NOTE: *This can be prepared up to 2 days ahead and refrigerated before baking. To bake, return to room temperature and follow baking directions.* ❧

PASTA, RICE, *and* GRAINS

MACARONI AND CHEESE

*T*his recipe, from the Canal House restaurant in New York City's Soho Grand Hotel, has been lifted from my last cookbook, *The New Elegant but Easy Cookbook*. Some things are worth repeating.

I have never met anyone who ate just one serving.

yield: 3 to 4 servings as a main dish
or 6 servings as a side dish

1 cup diced onion

2 tablespoons unsalted butter

2 tablespoons unbleached all-purpose flour

2 cups low-fat milk

1 tablespoon Dijon mustard

10 ounces extra-sharp aged white Cheddar, grated, PLUS 2 ounces, grated (see Sources, page 203)

Salt and freshly ground white pepper to taste

1/8 teaspoon ground nutmeg

1/4 to 1/2 teaspoon hot pepper sauce

8 ounces cavatappi (see Help Note, page 106)

2 tablespoons grated Parmigiano-Reggiano

1. In a large saucepan, cook the onion over low heat in the melted butter until the onion is soft but not browned, 5 to 7 minutes. Stir in the flour. Remove from the heat and whisk in the milk until thoroughly blended. Return to medium heat and cook, stirring, until the mixture *begins* to thicken. Remove from the heat and stir in the mustard and the 10 ounces of Cheddar, the salt, pepper, nutmeg, and hot pepper sauce.

2. Meanwhile, cook the cavatappi according to package directions until just al dente. Drain but do not rinse. Stir immediately into the prepared cheese sauce until well blended. Adjust the seasonings.

3. Spoon the mixture into a 9 by 13-inch baking dish. Top with the remaining 2 ounces of Cheddar and the Parmigiano-Reggiano.

4. Place the rack in the bottom third of oven. Preheat the oven to 400 degrees and bake for about 30 minutes, until the mixture is hot, bubbling throughout, and golden.

(continued)

HELP NOTE: *The finished casserole can be refrigerated before baking. To serve, let the dish return to room temperature and follow the directions in step 4.*

The quality and sharpness of the cheese are all-important to the success of this dish. Use a white Cheddar that has been aged at least 2 years. Grafton Village Cheese is always my choice (see Sources, page 203).

Other corkscrew pastas can be substituted for the cavatappi; the sauce adheres beautifully to this shape. ❦

MARINARA SAUCE FOR PASTA

*T*his is quick comfort food. The sauce got its name either because sailors had work to do and could not spend the day cooking it, or sailors' wives could make it quickly when they saw their husbands coming home. Take your pick.

yield: 4 servings

2 tablespoons olive oil
I very large onion (12 ounces or more), chopped
2 large cloves garlic, thinly sliced
5 cups canned plum tomatoes with their juice, pureed in a food processor

Salt and freshly ground black pepper to taste
I pound spaghetti or linguine
2 tablespoons chopped fresh thyme, oregano, and basil
Hot red pepper flakes, optional

1. Heat the olive oil in a deep pot. Sauté the onion over medium-high heat until it softens and takes on color. Add the garlic and watch carefully while it browns.

2. Bring water to a boil for the pasta in a covered pot.

3. Add the tomatoes and the salt and pepper to taste to the onion and garlic mixture and simmer over medium-high heat until the sauce bubbles; reduce the heat and cook 20 to 30 minutes.

4. Cook the pasta according to the package directions.

5. Add the herbs to the sauce and cook another 5 minutes. Add hot pepper flakes, if desired.

6. Serve over the drained pasta.

VARIATIONS: *To cook fish in the sauce, add ⅓ cup dry red or white wine for every cup of sauce, then add the fish and poach it in the sauce.*

Sauté ¾ pound of sliced mushrooms in the same pan as the onion after the onion has softened.

Add olives, capers, and/or anchovies in step 3.

Broil 2 sweet or hot Italian sausages; slice and add to the sauce in step 3.

You can use the sauce over breaded foods, like eggplant or chicken Parmesan or breaded veal.

WINE: *Zinfandel, Côtes du Rhône, Shiraz, Sangiovese, or Pinot Noir*

HELP NOTE: *This can be made ahead and refrigerated or frozen for a month.* ❧

LINGUINE WITH RED CLAM SAUCE

I love this dish at the shore, where clams are freshly dug. But you can make a fine version with clams from the fish market.

yield: 4 servings

48 littleneck clams
2 cups water
1 cup dry white wine
1 teaspoon dried oregano
3 sprigs parsley, PLUS 3 tablespoons chopped fresh parsley
1 pound fresh or dried linguine
3 tablespoons olive oil

4 cloves garlic, thinly sliced
2 cups diced ripe tomatoes
3 tablespoons chopped fresh basil
1 tablespoon chopped fresh oregano
1/4 teaspoon hot red pepper flakes
Salt and freshly ground black pepper to taste

1. Scrub the clams. Bring the 2 cups water, 1/2 cup wine, 1 teaspoon dried oregano, and the 3 sprigs parsley to a boil.

2. Add the clams, cover, and cook until the clams open, 2 or 3 minutes. Remove the clams as they open. Discard any that don't open. When they have all opened remove the pot from the heat. Pour the liquid through a fine strainer; remove the clams from their shells and cut them in half; set aside with the liquid. Discard the shells. Meanwhile, cook the linguine according to the package directions.

3. Clean out the pot in which the clams were cooked and dry it. Heat the oil, and sauté the garlic until it begins to brown, about 30 seconds. Add the tomatoes, chopped basil, remaining chopped parsley, fresh oregano, remaining 1/2 cup wine, and hot pepper flakes. Bring to a boil and cook a few minutes until the tomatoes soften.

4. Add the clams and the reserved liquid and cook about 2 minutes, until well blended. Season with the salt and pepper.

5. Add the cooked linguine to the pan, stir to coat, and serve.

WINE: *Chardonnay, Alsatian Pinot Gris, or Sauvignon Blanc, whichever you cook with*

HELP NOTE: *If you would prefer to have a large amount of clams and a small amount of pasta, reduce the linguine to ½ pound but keep the rest of the ingredients the same.*

If tomatoes are out of season, use cherry tomatoes with stems.

LOBSTER (ER, SHRIMP) FRA DIAVOLO

*J*ames Beard calls this the Italian version of lobster à l'Americaine. The rest of us call it a Boston or New York linguine dish. I was introduced to it when I went to college in the Boston area. Others are quite specific, attributing it to the North End of Boston. The only thing everyone agrees on is that this is not a dish from the old country.

Now that you know what it is, I have to tell you not too many people make it with lobster anymore—the cost of the crustacean keeps it from being just an ordinary meal found in the old red-checked-tablecloth restaurant with a candle in a Chianti bottle. So here's the shrimp version, with notes on how to make it with lobster, too.

yield: 4 servings

5 tablespoons olive oil
1 medium onion, finely chopped
3 very large cloves garlic, minced
1 tablespoon chopped fresh oregano
½ cup dry white wine
One 28-ounce can Italian plum tomatoes
1 teaspoon hot red pepper flakes, more
 or less

1 pound linguine
2 pounds fresh shrimp, peeled, tails left on
Salt and freshly ground black pepper
 to taste
1 tablespoon chopped fresh parsley

1. In a covered pot bring water to a boil for the linguine.

2. Heat the oil in a nonstick pan. Sauté the onion over medium-high heat until it begins to soften and color. Stir in the garlic and cook for 30 seconds. Add the oregano and wine and cook over high heat to reduce the wine by about one-third.

3. Add the tomatoes to the onion, crushing them in your hand before adding, along with their juice. Add the hot pepper to taste and cook over medium heat to reduce and thicken the mixture, about 15 minutes.

4. Cook the linguine according to package directions.

5. Add the shrimp to the sauce and cook for 2 or 3 minutes, until the shrimp is cooked but still tender. Season with the salt and pepper.

6. Serve the sauce over the linguine and sprinkle with the chopped parsley.

WINE: *Chardonnay, Alsatian Pinot Gris, or Sauvignon Blanc*

TO MAKE THE ORIGINAL LOBSTER FRA DIAVOLO (BROTHER DEVIL): *Prepare the sauce. While the sauce thickens, split two live 1¼-pound lobsters and clean. Break off the claws from the body and crack them slightly. Sear the claws in 3 tablespoons olive oil until the shells are bright red, 6 to 8 minutes. Remove the tail and discard the rest of the lobster. Add the tails and claws to the sauce. Cook over low heat until the meat is opaque, 10 to 15 minutes. Serve in the sauce, linguine on the side, if desired.*

James Beard added about ¼ cup cognac, very un-Italian-American, but very French, which is where he said the dish came from.

No one said this was a neat dish to eat. The lobster is served in the shells. Lots of napkins are in order along with the usual nutcrackers and picks. ❦

yield: 2 servings

RAGU OR MEAT SAUCE FOR SPAGHETTI

In an effort to find out how close my mother's version of meat sauce was to traditional Italian-American versions, I scoured the cookbooks available. Her recipe came from a woman who was cooking it at a picnic site in a park in Waterbury, Connecticut, where there was a large Italian immigrant population. The wonderful aromas prompted my mother to ask the woman how to make it.

The final adaptation contained green peppers and a bit of sugar to cut the acidity of the canned tomato. I haven't found any other sauces with green peppers, but who knows?

I used to have spaghetti and meat sauce once a week as a child, on Wednesday nights. There was always a little left over, and I liked it just as well cold and had it for breakfast Thursday morning.

I have been making variations on my mother's sauce ever since I began cooking, but no matter what I put in the ragu, it always reminds me of Wednesday nights in Waterbury.

yield: 4 to 6 servings

½ cup minced carrots
¾ pound onions, minced
2 thin slices pancetta, minced
2 tablespoons olive oil
2 large cloves garlic, minced
1 pound beef ground from a lean cut,
   like sirloin roast
½ cup full-bodied dry red wine

One 35-ounce can Italian plum tomatoes
   with basil
One 6-ounce can no-salt-added tomato
   paste
Salt and freshly ground black pepper
   to taste
1 pound spaghetti, cooked

1. Sauté the carrots, onions, and pancetta in the hot oil in a large, heavy-bottomed sauté pan over medium-high heat until the ingredients begin to take on color. Add the garlic and sauté for 30 seconds; remove the carrot mixture and set aside.

2. Brown the meat in the same pan over medium-high heat, stirring almost constantly to break the meat up into little pieces so it won't clump together.

3. When the meat is brown, add the wine and cook quickly until it is almost evaporated. Return the vegetables to the pan. Add the tomatoes and juices, breaking up the tomatoes with your fingers before adding them to the pan. Stir

in the tomato paste and season with the salt and pepper. Reduce the heat, cover the pan, and simmer for at least 1 hour; 2 hours is better. Adjust the seasonings.

4. Serve over the spaghetti.

WINE: *Shiraz, Côtes du Rhône, Zinfandel, or Sangiovese*

HELP NOTE: *I tried cooking the sauce for 3 hours but it didn't make it any better. This is a very thick sauce because there is no added water.*

For those who like hot pepper flakes, start with ¼ teaspoon and add with the tomatoes.

The best canned tomatoes are imported from San Marzano, Italy. Look for them on the Web. If you cannot find them, use no-salt-added tomatoes and season the sauce yourself. See Sources, page 204.

If you cannot find pancetta, substitute bacon.

This dish can easily be refrigerated for a couple of days. It also freezes very well for a month. Reheat to serve.

The Garlic Bread on page 136 is wonderful with this. ❦

MICHAEL'S EGGPLANT LASAGNA

$\mathcal{M}$y son, Michael Burros, owns a vegetarian restaurant in Santiago de Compostela, in Galicia in the northwest part of Spain. Called O Cabaliño do Demo, it has become a big hit.

This richly flavored lasagna will satisfy both carnivores and vegetarians.

This is the kind of dish you want to make when you need to cook to calm yourself. There are several steps and several hours involved in its preparation.

yield: 12 servings

TOMATO SAUCE
One 15-ounce package firm tofu
2 tablespoons soy sauce
2 medium-large onions, finely diced
¼ cup olive oil
1 large red bell pepper and 1 large green
   bell pepper, trimmed, seeded, and finely
   chopped

6 medium cloves garlic, finely minced
One 35-ounce can Italian plum tomatoes
¼ cup finely chopped fresh thyme or
   1 tablespoon dried
¼ cup finely chopped fresh oregano or
   1 tablespoon dried
¼ cup torn or chopped fresh basil
Salt and freshly ground black pepper

1. Drain the tofu and cut into ¼-inch pieces. Drizzle with soy sauce and freeze until firm, at least several hours or overnight.

2. Defrost the tofu and set aside.

3. Sauté the onions in the oil over medium-high heat until they soften and begin to brown.

4. Add the peppers and continue to sauté until the peppers soften.

5. Add the garlic and cook for 30 seconds over medium heat. Add the tofu without draining whatever juices have accumulated.

6. Add the tomatoes, crushing them in your hand before adding, along with the herbs. Simmer for 20 minutes until the mixture is thick. Season with the salt and pepper.

CHEESE, EGGPLANT, AND NOODLES

1½ pounds Fromage Blanc (see Help
    Note, page 116)
¾ cup grated Parmigiano-Reggiano
1 cup grated aged Gouda or sharp aged
    Cheddar
1 pound mushrooms, washed, trimmed,
    and sliced
1 tablespoon olive oil, PLUS additional oil
    for drizzling

1 large clove garlic, smashed
2 medium-small eggplant, trimmed but not
    peeled and sliced into ⅛-inch-thick
    rounds
Salt and freshly ground black pepper
    to taste
12 lasagna noodles, fresh or dried

1. Place a rack in the middle of the oven. Preheat the oven to 375 degrees.

2. Mix the Fromage Blanc with the Parmigiano-Reggiano and ¼ cup of Gouda. Set aside.

3. Sauté the mushrooms in 1 tablespoon oil over medium-high heat until they begin to brown.

4. Add the garlic and sauté 1 minute until the garlic begins to color. (Don't let it get too dark or it will be bitter.) Set the mushroom-garlic mixture aside.

5. Brush the eggplant slices on both sides with olive oil, season with the salt and pepper, and arrange on a baking sheet. Bake for about 30 minutes or until tender, turning once. Set aside.

6. Cook the lasagna according to package directions, rinse, and drizzle with oil so the noodles do not stick together.

BÉCHAMEL SAUCE

2 cups whole milk
1 bay leaf
1 large clove garlic, crushed
4 tablespoons (½ stick) unsalted butter or
    ¼ cup olive oil

¼ cup flour
2 teaspoons Dijon mustard
¾ teaspoon grated nutmeg
2 tablespoons dry sherry
Salt and white pepper to taste

1. In a pot, heat the milk just until bubbles appear at the edge. Remove from the heat, add the bay leaf and garlic, and steep for 20 minutes.

(continued)

2. Melt the butter or olive oil in a deep pot. Remove from the heat and whisk in the flour. Return the pot to the stove and cook over low heat a couple of minutes to get rid of the floury taste.

3. Remove from the heat. Discard the garlic and bay leaf from the milk. Slowly whisk the milk into the flour-butter mixture, whisking constantly to avoid lumps.

4. Return to the heat and cook until thickened. Remove from the heat and add the mustard, nutmeg, sherry, salt, and pepper. Stir in the reserved mushroom-garlic mixture.

ASSEMBLING THE LASAGNA

1. In a 9 by 13-inch pan, place a small amount of the tomato sauce on the bottom.

2. Top with a single layer of noodles.

3. Place the eggplant on top of the noodles and spoon half the remaining tomato sauce on top.

4. Place another layer of noodles on the sauce and top with the cheese mixture.

5. Add another layer of noodles and top with the mushroom-béchamel sauce.

6. Add another layer of noodles and top with the remaining tomato sauce. Sprinkle with the remaining ¾ cup Gouda.

7. Bake for about 45 minutes, until browned and bubbling. Allow to rest for 10 minutes before cutting.

WINE: *Sangiovese, light Cabernet Franc, or light Zinfandel*

HELP NOTE: *The tofu is frozen first because it holds its shape better. Do this the night before.*

The lasagna can be refrigerated or frozen up to a month if desired. Be sure to wrap well. To serve, return to room temperature, uncover, and follow baking directions.

Susan Simon, who retested this recipe for me, made this suggestion: Since this is quite a bit of work, why not make three or four at a time? They freeze beautifully, and it really would not take much longer.

Fromage Blanc can be found in many supermarkets and natural food stores. See Sources, page 203. ❧

FRIED RICE

$\mathcal{F}$ried rice was a childhood treat and probably one of the few authentic Chinese dishes I ate then. Most of my consumption was chop suey and chow mein, with an occasional sub gum.

yield: 2 servings

2 tablespoons oil
4 eggs, beaten with a few shakes of salt
¼ cup small peeled shrimp, slit in half
  lengthwise and cut in ¼-inch pieces
½ cup diced cooked chicken breast
½ cup diced cooked roast pork (leftover
  Chinese roast pork is good)

¼ cup frozen peas
3 cups cold cooked long-grain rice
2 green onions, chopped
Salt to taste
1 cup assorted baby salad greens or baby
  spinach

1. Heat 1 tablespoon of the oil in a skillet and over medium heat cook the eggs as for an omelet, pushing the cooked eggs back and allowing the raw eggs to fill in and cook. Repeat until the mixture is cooked. Remove and shred.

2. Clean out the pan and add the remaining oil. Quickly cook the shrimp over medium-high heat, just until pink. Remove. Add the chicken, pork, and peas and cook long enough to heat the peas through. Add the shrimp and stir for 1 minute.

3. Add the rice, green onions, salt, and eggs and stir well to heat all the ingredients. Stir in the greens and mix for about 30 seconds.

HELP NOTE: *Fried rice is a perfect vehicle for leftovers; you can use any meats or seafood, mushrooms, or peppers. The only constant ingredient in fried rice is the rice.*

The one inauthentic ingredient I have substituted is the greens for the bean sprouts. I'm inclined to stay away from all sprouts these days because they breed the kind of bacteria that can make you sick; in this recipe they are not cooked enough to kill the bacteria. But if you want to use bean sprouts, you could try canned sprouts (though I find they have a tinny taste); the canning process removes the hazardous bacteria. The fresh taste of the greens, however, is much preferred.

Not every version of fried rice contains soy sauce; the Cantonese version, with which most Americans are familiar, does. I prefer the dish without because it has a clean, bright taste, but if you want to add soy sauce, 1 to 2 tablespoons should be about right. 🌿

RISOTTO

*C*ontrary to much cooking information, risotto does not take 40 minutes to prepare; it's closer to 25.

Other rice varieties appropriate for risotto include vialone and carnaroli.

yield: 4 side servings or 2 main-course servings

4 cups good-quality stock (chicken, vegetable, beef, or fish), approximately
4 tablespoons olive oil or unsalted butter
½ cup minced onion
1 cup arborio rice

½ cup dry white wine
Salt and freshly ground black pepper to taste
1 cup grated Parmigiano-Reggiano

1. Bring the stock to a boil in a 2-quart pot; reduce the heat and keep at a low simmer.

2. In another pan, heat the oil, add the onion, and cook over medium-high heat until the onion is translucent.

3. Stir the rice into the onion and mix until the rice is evenly coated. Reduce the heat to low. Add the white wine and stir until the liquid is absorbed. Add the hot stock, about ⅔ cup at a time, stirring very frequently until the liquid is absorbed. Repeat until the rice is creamy but still firm to the tooth (al dente) and all the stock (or most of the stock) has been used. Season with the salt and pepper.

4. Stir in the Parmigiano-Reggiano, and serve immediately. 🌿

MAKE-AHEAD RISOTTO

This is what chefs do in Italian restaurants so that you don't have to wait forever when you order risotto.

In a 2-quart pot, bring 2 cups of the stock to a boil and follow the rest of the directions through part of step 3 (page 118), only until the 2 cups of stock have been absorbed. Pour the risotto onto a cookie sheet or jelly roll pan. This will stop the cooking and cool the rice as quickly as possible. Refrigerate, uncovered, until the rice is cold. The rice can be stored for up to 2 days in a covered plastic container.

To finish the risotto, bring 1½ cups stock to a boil.

Place the chilled risotto in a 4-quart pot over medium heat and add ¼ pound unsalted butter.

Pour the boiling stock slowly into the risotto, stirring constantly with a wooden spoon. Continue cooking until the rice is just barely tender but still al dente. Season with the salt and pepper. If the risotto is too thick, add a little more stock.

Stir in the Parmigiano-Reggiano, and serve immediately.

GARLIC CHEESE GRITS

Grits came to Washington, D.C., where I live, with the Carter administration. Everyone wanted to be the first on the block to serve them, but as soon as the Carters left grits went back to being a Southern dish.

Thanks for this recipe go to Tom Head, executive food editor and restaurant critic of *The Washingtonian*, the city magazine for Washington, D.C. It has been adapted but very little is changed.

yield: 6 to 8 servings

4 cups water
½ teaspoon salt
1 cup uncooked grits
8 tablespoons (1 stick) unsalted butter
½ pound extra-sharp Cheddar, grated
   (see Sources, page 203)

1 teaspoon finely minced garlic
1½ teaspoons Worcestershire sauce
Paprika

1. Place the water and salt in a saucepan and bring to a boil over medium heat. Stir the grits into the boiling water and cook slowly until the mixture thickens, about 30 minutes.

2. Place a rack in the middle of the oven. Preheat the oven to 350 degrees. Grease a 1½-quart casserole.

3. Add the butter, Cheddar, garlic, and Worcestershire sauce to the grits and stir until melted.

4. Spoon the grits into the prepared casserole, sprinkle with paprika, and bake for 15 to 20 minutes, until the mixture is bubbling.

HELP NOTE: *The grits can be prepared ahead and refrigerated overnight. To serve, return to room temperature and bake as directed.*

Tom Head explained (and I have since heard this from others) that all Southern cooks know this recipe. However, as soon as they leave the South they can't find the rolls of garlic-flavored cheese thought to be essential for this dish so they improvise, substituting Cheddar and garlic. I'm happy to use the best extra-sharp Cheddar (Grafton Village Cheese is my choice, see Sources, page 203) and fresh garlic.

Please don't use instant grits. 🌿

POLENTA

*T*here's polenta and there's instant polenta; until I went to Friuli, Italy, the home of polenta, I always cooked the instant version. It's good, and especially good for quick meals. But after experiencing the creaminess of long-cooking polenta, I'm convinced that when you have the time, it's worth the effort.

yield: 10 to 12 servings

9 cups water	4 teaspoons olive oil
2 cups regular polenta	Salt to taste

1. Bring the water to a boil in a heavy pot.

2. Slowly stir in the polenta, whisking constantly to prevent lumps from forming. Add the olive oil and salt. Reduce the heat so that the polenta bubbles just break the surface.

3. *Do not stir.* Cook for about 40 minutes, until the polenta has thickened and the water has been absorbed.

4. Serve immediately, plain or with butter, cheese, or sauce.

5. You can also pour the polenta into a shallow 10 by 15-inch baking dish and allow to set. Cover with the desired topping and refrigerate. To serve, place a rack in the middle of the oven and preheat the oven to 350 degrees. Bake the polenta about 30 minutes to heat through.

HELP NOTE: *It is heresy to suggest cooking polenta without stirring it constantly, but I learned this trick at Al Covo, a marvelous small restaurant in Venice owned by an Italian, Caesare Bellini, and his Texas-born wife, Diane. "We never stir polenta," she said. "We let a crust form, and after we remove the polenta we soak the pot and the crust comes right off." And it does. The polenta is so creamy, I can't imagine why it should be cooked any other way, but I know I will get a lot of arguments from Italian and Italian-American cooks.*

VEGETABLES
and SIDES

GREEN BEANS AMANDINE

*T*he first green beans amandine I remember were made with frozen green beans, no onion, and no mushrooms, so maybe this isn't Green Beans Amandine anymore: it's something much more savory. The sweetness of the onions and almonds and the earthiness of the mushrooms are a nice balance for the beans. The onions are cooked until they are almost caramelized.

yield: 6 to 8 servings

1 pound onions, peeled
3 tablespoons neutral vegetable oil, such as canola
½ cup sliced almonds
¾ pound portobello mushrooms, trimmed and cut in ½-inch dice

2 pounds haricots verts or young tender green beans, trimmed
Salt to taste

1. Process the onions using the 2-millimeter blade of a food processor. Place in a clean towel and squeeze out as much liquid as possible.

2. Heat the oil in a large saucepan; do not use a nonstick pan. Reduce the heat to medium-high and sauté the onions in the oil, stirring often. When the onions have partially browned, reduce the heat to medium; stir in the almonds and continue sautéing until the almonds begin to brown.

3. Add the mushrooms and cook 3 or 4 minutes. Set aside.

4. Steam the haricots verts over boiling water for 7 to 10 minutes, until the beans are tender but still firm. Drain and stir into the onion mix. Season with salt.

VARIATION: *For color add 1 roasted red pepper cut into julienne strips.*

HELP NOTE: *If you have access to garden-fresh green beans, I recommend them wholeheartedly. However, the beans you usually find in the supermarket are so old and tough that I spend the extra money on haricots verts, the thin green beans with a delicate flavor.*

The onion mix can be prepared a day ahead and refrigerated. Reheat with a little additional oil before combining with the haricots verts. 🌿

"OVEN FRIED" ZUCCHINI

Somewhere between deep-fried and boiled, this way of cooking zucchini brings out the sweetness of the vegetable, though it does not provide the same crispness as cooking in hot fat does. These belong in the streamlined category.

yield: 4 servings

Olive oil pan spray
1 cup flour
1 cup water
2 tablespoons oil

Salt to taste
2 egg whites
2 large zucchini, trimmed and cut ⅛ inch thick

1. Place a rack in the top third of the oven. Preheat the oven to 450 degrees. Spray a nonstick baking sheet with pan spray.

2. In a bowl, mix the flour with the water, oil, and salt. Let stand for 20 minutes.

3. Beat the egg whites until soft peaks form; then fold into the batter. Dip each zucchini slice in the batter and place on the prepared pan. Roast about 10 minutes, until the slices are browned on the bottoms, then turn and roast a few minutes longer.

HELP NOTE: Unlike potatoes, zucchini are filled with water, so roasting at high heat only softens them. A coating is needed to provide crispness and brown them. Flour provides the brownness; egg whites help the coating stick to the slices. A streamlined dish.

The zucchini are delicious plain, but a dill- or curry-flavored yogurt sauce would be a nice accompaniment. 🌿

CAULIFLOWER PUREE

*I*t's amazing what happens to the subtle flavor of cauliflower when you dress it up with nutmeg, cardamom, and mace and top it off with plenty of butter. It assumes star qualities.

yield: 6 to 8 servings

4 pounds cauliflower
5 tablespoons unsalted butter
¼ teaspoon ground nutmeg

¼ teaspoon ground cardamom
⅛ teaspoon ground mace
Salt and white pepper to taste

1. Remove the leaves and core from the cauliflower and break it into florets. Steam over boiling water until quite tender but not mushy, about 5 minutes. Drain thoroughly.

2. Put the cauliflower in the food processor with the butter and process to a puree in two or three batches. Spoon the puree into a bowl. Season with the nutmeg, cardamom, mace, salt, and pepper and stir well.

HELP NOTE: The cauliflower can be made up to a day ahead and reheated very slowly in the top of a double boiler over hot water.

Less than a tablespoon of butter per serving puts this dish in the streamlined category. ✻

CARROT PUREE

*W*hen my children were small, I could get them to eat almost anything if I made it into an hors d'oeuvre. The same was true for rich, buttery vegetable purees.

yield: 4 servings

1 pound carrots, peeled and cut into
  ½-inch cubes
1 medium-large potato, peeled, sliced
  ⅛ inch thick, slices cut ¼ inch wide

2 teaspoons finely chopped fresh thyme
1 tablespoon unsalted butter
2 tablespoons milk
Salt and white pepper to taste

1. In a covered pot, boil the carrots and potato together in water to cover for 10 to 15 minutes, until the vegetables are soft. Drain.

2. Spoon the vegetables into a food processor with the thyme, butter, and milk, and process to a puree. Season with the salt and pepper.

HELP NOTE: *This dish can be made in advance, refrigerated overnight, and reheated slowly in the top of double boiler over hot water.*

When I made this recipe for the first time I used 1 percent milk, because that is what was in the house. It falls in the streamlined category. You could easily make the dish richer by using heavy cream or half-and-half. No matter what you use, the puree tastes quite creamy. 🌿

ROASTED POTATOES

*W*hat we've all finally discovered is that you don't have to have a standing rib roast in order to have delicious roasted potatoes, and you definitely don't have to peel them. In fact, you shouldn't.

yield: 6 servings

2 to 3 tablespoons olive oil

2 tablespoons chopped fresh rosemary, thyme, marjoram, or sage

Salt and freshly ground black pepper to taste

2 pounds tiny new potatoes, 1 inch to 1½ inches in diameter, scrubbed and halved

1. Place a rack in the top third of the oven. Preheat the oven to 425 degrees.

2. Mix the oil with the herbs, salt, and pepper. Coat the potatoes with the oil mixture and arrange in a single layer in a shallow baking pan, like a jelly roll pan, cut side down. Roast 20 to 30 minutes, turning after 15 minutes, until they are lightly browned and cooked through.

HELP NOTE: *The wonderful thing about Roasted Potatoes is that you can also bake them at 375 or 400 degrees to accommodate whatever else you may have in the oven. Adjust the time to the temperature accordingly.*

Use low-starch or waxy potatoes like Yukon Gold, Red Bliss, Yellow Finn, or fingerlings. These have a higher moisture content, so they are creamier and softer than Russets, for example.

If you can't find tiny new potatoes, use larger ones and cut them in cubes or in slices. A streamlined dish. ❧

MASHED POTATOES

$\mathcal{W}$hat did you do with mashed potatoes as a child? Make indentations in which to spoon the gravy? Spoon them over the meat loaf or hamburger? Divide them into small piles and eat each one separately?

No matter how rich your mashed potatoes were, I'll bet your mother never made them with Crème Fraîche (page 167).

yield: 6 to 8 servings

2 pounds (4 large) Yukon Gold or other boiling potatoes
2/3 cup half-and-half
1/2 cup Crème Fraîche (page 167; or see Sources, page 203)

6 tablespoons (3/4 stick) very soft unsalted butter
Salt and white pepper to taste

1. Scrub the potatoes. Cover them with cold water and boil them until tender (they should still hold their shape). Drain the potatoes and peel them.

2. Warm the half-and-half and Crème Fraîche in a saucepan over low heat.

3. Mash the potatoes with a potato masher and add the butter. Mix well and stir in the cream mixture. Season with the salt and pepper.

VARIATION: *Garlic Mashed Potatoes: Using 2 of the 6 tablespoons butter in the recipe, sauté four minced cloves of garlic over very low heat until very soft; do not brown. Use the rest of the butter for mashing. Mix the garlic into the potatoes and then add the half-and-half mixture.*

HELP NOTE: *Do not mash the potatoes in a food processor or blender; the gluten in the potatoes will develop and make the mixture gummy.*

The potatoes can be made a day ahead if absolutely necessary and reheated very slowly on top of the stove. Or they can be placed in a glass dish, covered with plastic wrap, and reheated in the microwave about 8 minutes on high. Stir once or twice while reheating. If the potatoes become too dry, stir in additional half-and-half. They are at their very best freshly made. ❦

STREAMLINED MASHED POTATOES

*S*ince people always ask for seconds when I serve these potatoes, I see no reason to tell them they are made with buttermilk until after they have eaten them.

yield: 6 servings

2 pounds unpeeled thin-skinned potatoes (Yukon Gold or other boiling potatoes) scrubbed and sliced ¼ inch thick

2 cups nonfat buttermilk, or more
Salt and freshly ground black pepper to taste

1. Cook the potato slices in water to cover until tender, about 10 minutes. Do not let them get so soft that they start to disintegrate; that makes them watery. Drain and mash the potatoes—peel and all—in a food mill, through a ricer, or with a potato masher.

2. Stir in the buttermilk until the potatoes become creamy. Season with salt and pepper.

HELP NOTE: *The potatoes can be refrigerated if they are well covered, but they are best when fresh. To serve, place in a glass dish, cover with plastic wrap, and reheat in the microwave for about 8 minutes on high. Stir once or twice while reheating. If the potatoes become too dry, stir in additional buttermilk.*

Use waxy potatoes for boiling like Red Bliss or fingerlings. Yukon Golds are all-purpose. ❦

TWICE-BAKED POTATOES

*T*hese were a staple of the 1950s and 1960s, served with steak. You know you have reached twice-baked-potato Nirvana when you scoop out a forkful of potato and you can see the melted cheese glistening.

yield: 8 potato halves

4 large baking potatoes, such as Russets
Oil for rubbing potatoes
8 ounces finely grated extra-sharp
   Cheddar (2 cups) (see Sources,
   page 203)

½ cup sour cream, or more
2 teaspoons Dijon mustard
4 tablespoons minced fresh chives
Salt and freshly ground black pepper
   to taste

1. Place a rack in the lower third of the oven. Preheat the oven to 400 degrees.

2. Scrub potatoes and rub lightly with oil.

3. Bake the potatoes for 45 minutes to 1 hour, depending on their size.

4. Remove the potatoes from the oven and then reduce the oven temperature to 375 degrees. As soon as the potatoes are cool enough to handle, cut them in half lengthwise and scoop out the flesh into a pot. Mash with a potato masher and mix to a creamy consistency with the Cheddar, sour cream, mustard, chives, salt, and pepper.

5. Spoon the filling into each potato half. Bake until the tops begin to brown, 10 to 15 minutes.

HELP NOTE: *The potatoes may be prepared ahead through step 4. Cover and refrigerate. To serve, preheat the oven to 375 degrees. Return the potatoes to room temperature for 30 minutes and follow the directions in step 5.*

If you want to make the potatoes look a little fancier, press the stuffed filling with a fork to make lines and decorate with very, very thin strips of red and yellow roasted peppers. 🌱

CLASSIC POTATO SALAD

I'd rather eat the potato salad than anything else at the picnic, so I offer two versions. But I want a version that has only enough celery to add the necessary crunch, and I want it cut into very, very small pieces so it isn't obvious.

yield: 8 to 10 servings

2½ pounds Red Bliss or Yukon Gold
    potatoes, unpeeled
6 eggs
1 cup mayonnaise
½ cup finely chopped red onion
½ cup finely diced celery

6 tablespoons minced cornichons
3 tablespoons red wine vinegar
2 tablespoons Dijon mustard
Salt and freshly ground black pepper
    to taste

1. Scrub the potatoes, cover with water, and bring to a boil. Cook until tender but still firm. Cooking time will depend on the size of the potatoes, but it should be between 20 and 30 minutes. (Don't let them get mushy.) Drain and set aside.

2. Hard-cook the eggs: place them in a pot of cold water, bring to a boil, and boil for 3 minutes. Remove the pot from the heat and allow the eggs to sit in the water, covered, for 20 minutes. Run the eggs under cold water until they are cooled. Shell and coarsely chop the eggs.

3. In a bowl, combine the mayonnaise, onion, celery, cornichons, vinegar, and mustard. Cut the potatoes into ½-inch pieces. Do not peel them. Gently mix in the potatoes while they are still warm. Gently mix in the eggs, season with salt and pepper, and serve.

HELP NOTE: *The salad can be served immediately or it can be covered and refrigerated overnight.*

New potatoes take less time to cook.

There is no reason to peel the potatoes; their skins are so thin, they add nice texture and color to the salad.

If you use a serrated knife to cut the potatoes, the skins won't tear.

Cornichons are tiny French pickles with a sharp, vinegary taste and no sweetness at all. They are available in specialty markets and some large supermarkets.

For a streamlined version of the potato salad, use light mayonnaise, 3 whole eggs, and 6 egg whites. ❦

POTATO AND FENNEL SALAD

*F*or a change of pace from the classic potato salad, substitute fennel for the celery. It provides the crunch and a bonus: the assertive flavor of anise.

yield: 4 servings

1 pound Red Bliss or Yukon Gold potatoes	1 teaspoon fennel seeds
4 eggs	½ cup mayonnaise
1 small head fennel (to yield heaping ¼ cup)	2 teaspoons Dijon mustard
	Few shakes salt
3 green onions	Freshly ground black pepper to taste

1. Scrub the potatoes (do not peel) and cook in boiling water to cover, about 20 to 30 minutes, depending on their size. (Do not allow to become mushy or they become watery.)

2. Hard-cook the eggs by placing them in cold water and bringing to a boil. Boil for 3 minutes. Remove from the heat and allow them to sit in the water, covered, for 20 minutes. Then run the eggs under cold water until they are cooled.

3. Wash, trim, and mince the fennel. Wash the green onions and trim and finely slice the white and the light part of the green. Place the fennel, green onions, fennel seeds, mayonnaise, and mustard in a serving bowl.

4. Cut the reserved potatoes into small dice—do not peel—and add to the bowl. Peel and coarsely chop the eggs and gently stir them into the potato mixture. Season with the salt and pepper.

HELP NOTE: *The salad can be served as soon as it is prepared or it can be covered and refrigerated overnight.*

If you are using new potatoes, they take less time to cook.

For streamlined potato salad substitute light mayonnaise for regular. 🌿

CRANBERRY ORANGE RELISH

I must have cranberries at Thanksgiving dinner. When the turkey is dry, the cranberry sauce makes it go down more easily and actually makes it taste good. It's the tartness of this recipe that I find so appealing, a very strong contrast to the usual dishes on a Thanksgiving table. Comfort food? Definitely.

yield: about 3 cups

2 cups fresh cranberries
2 oranges, pitted, peel removed from
    1 orange
6 heaping tablespoons toasted chopped
    pecans
6 tablespoons dried cranberries

6 tablespoons maple syrup
2 tablespoons Grand Marnier (see Help
    Note below)
2 tablespoons sugar
¼ teaspoon ground nutmeg

1. Wash and pick over the cranberries. Grind them in a meat grinder using the fine blade, or process in a food processor until the cranberries are finely chopped. Place the cranberries in a large bowl.

2. Cut the oranges into eighths and grind or process until finely chopped.

3. Combine the cranberries, oranges, pecans, dried cranberries, maple syrup, Grand Marnier, sugar, and nutmeg. Stir well and refrigerate at least an hour or up to 3 or 4 days.

HELP NOTE: A grinder provides a more consistent texture than the food processor.
Any orange liqueur is fine. ❦

GARLIC BREAD

*T*his recipe is inspired by the garlic bread of my youth, but it is infinitely better. Much better to cook the garlic.

yield: 6 servings

2 tablespoons olive oil
1 to 3 cloves garlic, mashed
4 tablespoons (½ stick) unsalted butter

2 tablespoons chopped fresh parsley
One 1-pound baguette

1. Set the rack in the middle of the oven. Preheat the oven to 400 degrees.

2. Heat the oil in a small saucepan over low heat. Cook the garlic in the oil until it is soft, to remove the bitter raw taste. Do not let the garlic color.

3. Remove the garlic from the heat and stir in the butter in thin slices. Mix to melt completely. Stir in the parsley.

4. Slice the baguette lengthwise and spread the garlic mixture over the cut surfaces. Place the bread on a baking sheet cut sides up, and bake for 15 to 20 minutes, until the butter begins to bubble and brown.

HELP NOTE: *To prepare ahead, wrap the unbaked garlic bread in foil and refrigerate overnight, if desired. To serve, unwrap and bake as directed.*

If a garlic clove has a green sprout in the middle, at the very least discard the sprout; it's bitter. 🍃

JALAPEÑO CORN BREAD PUDDING

*Y*ears ago, when I was looking for a dressing for the Thanksgiving turkey, something moister and tastier than the white bread dressings I was familiar with, I came upon a Southern dressing that intrigued me because it called for corn bread.

I tried it, and when the bread was baked, I couldn't resist sampling a piece before I added the rest of the ingredients for the dressing. It was a revelation; so much more interesting and so much moister than the traditional corn breads I had been served since moving below the Mason Dixon line. It's really closer to a pudding.

I'm a convert and my version is what converted me.

yield: 25 pieces about 2 by 3 inches, or 7 or 8 cups of cubes

Two 8½-ounce cans or 2 cups PLUS
   2 tablespoons cream-style corn
2 cups stone-ground yellow cornmeal
4 lightly beaten eggs
¾ to 1 teaspoon salt
1 teaspoon baking soda

2 cups buttermilk
⅔ cup corn oil
2 cups grated Monterey Jack
1 teaspoon to 1 tablespoon minced
   jalapeño
2 tablespoons unsalted butter

1. Place a rack in the middle of the oven and preheat the oven to 400 degrees.

2. Combine the corn, cornmeal, eggs, salt, baking soda, buttermilk, corn oil, Monterey Jack, and jalapeño and mix well.

3. Put the butter in a 10 by 15-inch baking pan and put it in the oven for about 5 minutes to melt. Remove from the oven and pour in the batter. Bake about 30 minutes, until the corn bread begins to pull away from the sides of the pan and a knife inserted near the center of the pan comes out clean.

4. Serve immediately, or turn into Jalapeño Corn Bread Stuffing (page 138).

HELP NOTE: Be sure to use stone-ground cornmeal; it has a better texture and more "corny" taste.

Any kind of buttermilk works, from whole to nonfat. 🌶

JALAPEÑO CORN BREAD STUFFING

yield: enough to stuff a 12- to 14-pound turkey, about 14 cups

5 cups Jalapeño Corn Bread cubes
  (page 137)
5 cups toasted bread cubes, your choice
  of type
2 hard-cooked eggs, chopped
2 tablespoons butter
2 cups finely chopped onions
2 large cloves garlic, minced

1½ cups chopped green bell peppers
1 cup finely minced celery
Salt and freshly ground black pepper
  to taste
3 lightly beaten eggs
½ cup good-quality chicken stock
  (approximately)

1. Combine the corn bread, bread cubes, and chopped eggs in a large bowl; mix lightly. Set aside.

2. Melt the butter in a large skillet and sauté the onions over medium heat until they have softened. Add the garlic and sauté 30 seconds more. Add the peppers and celery and cook until tender but still crisp. Season with the salt and pepper. Cool slightly.

3. Add the onion mixture to the corn bread mixture, blending well. Stir in the beaten eggs and enough stock to moisten lightly.

HELP NOTE: *Don't stuff your turkey with warm dressing unless you are roasting it immediately. The stuffing can be made a day ahead, chilled in the refrigerator, and then used to stuff the turkey in advance of roasting.*

   There will be some corn bread left over from the recipe. Have it for dinner. 🌿

DESSERTS

COOKIES *and* BARS

GRAMMIE LANG'S PECAN COOKIES

*S*usan Simon, who did a lot of testing for this book, says these are her favorite cookies—or at least they were until she tried some Shortbread Cookies (see page 145). These literally melt in your mouth and are chock full of pecans.

yield: approximately 3 dozen cookies

16 tablespoons (2 sticks) unsalted butter, softened	2 cups sifted cake flour
1 cup sifted confectioners' sugar	1 tablespoon pure vanilla extract
	1 cup coarsely chopped toasted pecans

1. In an electric mixer, beat the butter until light. Add the confectioners' sugar gradually, and cream until very, very light and fluffy.

2. On the lowest mixer speed, gradually add the flour and mix thoroughly. Add the vanilla and stir in the toasted pecans. The batter will be quite stiff. Refrigerate for an hour or longer.

3. Place racks in the middle of the oven. Preheat the oven to 350 degrees.

4. Drop batter by rounded teaspoonfuls onto ungreased cookie sheets, about 1½ inches apart. Bake 12 to 15 minutes, or until the edges of the cookies are golden brown. Cool on the cookie sheets a few minutes and then transfer to wire racks until completely cool.

5. Store in a tightly covered container for a few days or freeze for up to a month.

HELP NOTE: The dough can also be formed into a log, wrapped well, and frozen for up to a month for future use. To serve, defrost, slice, and bake as directed. ❦

CARYN'S MOLASSES COOKIES

*B*efore Caryn Brooks became Caryn Coleman, she sent her soon-to-be father-in-law, Roy Coleman (my significant other), a couple of her molasses cookies and asked him to let me taste one. That's when I knew her husband-to-be, David, was going to eat well. These soft, chewy cookies are redolent of old-fashioned spicy flavors, and Caryn was kind enough to share the recipe for them.

yield: about thirty 2-inch cookies

12 tablespoons (1½ sticks) unsalted butter, melted and slightly cooled
1 cup granulated sugar
¼ cup dark molasses
1 slightly beaten egg
Scant ½ cup chopped crystallized ginger pieces

2 cups unbleached all-purpose flour
2 teaspoons baking soda
½ teaspoon ground ginger
½ teaspoon ground cloves
¼ to ½ teaspoon plus salt
Additional sugar, Demerara (if you can find it) or granulated, for rolling the cookies

1. Mix the butter with the 1 cup granulated sugar and the molasses and blend thoroughly.

2. Stir in the egg and crystallized ginger.

3. In a bowl, stir together the flour, baking soda, ginger, cloves, and salt. Add them to the butter mixture and blend well. Chill the dough for several hours in the refrigerator or for about 30 minutes in the freezer so that it is firm enough to shape into balls.

4. Place the racks in the middle of the oven. Preheat the oven to 375 degrees. Grease two cookie sheets or place Silpat mats (see Help Note, page 143) on them.

5. Spoon some Demerara sugar into a large plastic bag. Shape the dough into 1-inch balls and shake several balls at a time in the sugar to coat. Arrange the balls on cookie sheets about an inch apart. (The cookies spread to 2 inches.)

6. Bake 8 to 10 minutes, depending on how soft you want the middle. I prefer 10 minutes in my oven so the cookies get soft but not doughy. Remove from the oven, cool a few minutes on the cookie sheets, and then remove and cool completely.

HELP NOTE: *The cookies should have little cracks on the edges when they are baked. They will keep at room temperature in a tightly covered box for a week. They can also be frozen for a month.*

Demerara sugar is coarser than granulated sugar and will show up a little better on the finished cookies, but there is no difference in taste.

Silpat mats are great for turning traditional cookie sheets into nonstick surfaces. You can put the mats in the dishwasher and roll them up; just don't cut them. If you can't find them in your local kitchenware shop, you can order them on-line. See Sources, page 204. 🌱

RAISIN NUT OATMEAL COOKIES

I always feel virtuous eating these cookies: oatmeal, raisins, nuts! But they can also be made without the raisins and nuts.

yield: about 4 dozen cookies

3 cups oatmeal

1½ cups unbleached all-purpose flour

¼ teaspoon salt

1 teaspoon baking powder

1 teaspoon ground cinnamon

¼ teaspoon ground nutmeg

½ pound plus 4 tablespoons (2½ sticks) unsalted butter

1 cup firmly packed dark brown sugar

½ cup granulated sugar

2 eggs plus 1 egg yolk

4 teaspoons pure vanilla extract

1½ cups raisins, optional

1½ cups chopped walnuts, optional

1. Place the rack in the middle of the oven. Preheat the oven to 350 degrees. Lightly grease two cookie sheets or use Silpat nonstick mats (see Help Note below).

2. Combine the oatmeal, flour, salt, baking powder, cinnamon, and nutmeg.

3. In an electric mixer, cream the butter. Add the sugars and beat 2 to 3 minutes until the mixture is the consistency of wet sand. Add the eggs, egg yolk, and vanilla, and beat well.

4. Add the oat-flour mixture and beat well.

5. Add the raisins and nuts, if using, and beat well.

6. Drop the dough by rounded teaspoonfuls onto the prepared cookie sheets and bake for 13 to 15 minutes, until golden brown. Remove and cool on racks.

HELP NOTE: *The oatmeal can be regular or quick-cooking.*

For a softer, chewier cookie bake a few minutes less. For a crisp cookie bake a few minutes more.

Cookies can be baked and frozen for a month, if desired. Wrap well. Otherwise, keep the cookies at room temperature in a tightly covered container. See Sources, page 204, for Silpat mats. ❦

SHORTBREAD COOKIES

*T*he best shortbread cookies both crumble and melt in your mouth. And their flavor is pure butter.

yield: about 50 cookies

I pound unsalted butter, softened
I cup superfine sugar
3 cups unbleached all-purpose flour
I cup white rice flour (see Help Note below)

Confectioners' sugar for sprinkling
Granulated sugar for rolling

1. In an electric mixer, cream the butter until light and fluffy. Gradually add the superfine sugar and beat to cream thoroughly.

2. Blend the flours. Sift over the creamed mixture, a little at a time, beating well after each addition.

3. Lightly dust two sheets of wax paper with some confectioners' sugar. Form the dough into 1½-inch cylinders on the wax paper and refrigerate a few hours or freeze to firm up.

4. Set the racks near the middle of the oven. Preheat the oven to 350 degrees.

5. To make the cookies, roll the dough in granulated sugar to coat the edges and cut into ¼-inch slices. Place ½ inch apart on ungreased cookie sheets and bake for 10 minutes. Reduce the temperature to 300 degrees and bake for about 15 to 20 minutes longer, until the cookies are light golden but not browned. Remove from the sheets and cool on a rack.

HELP NOTE: *The powdered sugar keeps the dough from sticking.*

Rice flour is available at health food stores; see also Sources, page 203.

If you can't find rice flour, substitute another cup of all-purpose flour. The cookies won't be quite as delicate but they are still addictive.

If you want a prettier cookie, allow the chilled dough to soften slightly. Roll out the dough to ⅜ inch thick. Cut the dough with a 1½-inch scalloped round cookie cutter. Sprinkle with granulated sugar, place rounds ½ inch apart on ungreased cookie sheets, and bake as directed above. ❦

PEANUT BUTTER COOKIES

The idea of putting ganache inside a sandwich of peanut butter cookies comes from Best Buns Bread Company of Arlington, Virginia, which provided the peanut butter cookie recipe that I have adapted. These are big, soft cookies, my favorite kind. One cookie sandwich is more than enough for one person.

yield: 24 cookies; 12 cookie sandwiches

1 cup PLUS 2 tablespoons smooth natural peanut butter

16 tablespoons (2 sticks) unsalted butter, softened

1½ cups minus 1 tablespoon sugar, PLUS additional sugar for sprinkling

2 eggs

1 teaspoon pure vanilla extract

2⅓ cups unbleached all-purpose flour

2 teaspoons baking soda

¾ teaspoon salt

6 ounces dry-roasted unsalted peanuts

Ganache (see recipe, page 147)

1. Place racks near the middle of the oven. Preheat the oven to 350 degrees.

2. Using an electric mixer, cream together the peanut butter and butter. Add the 1½ cups minus 1 tablespoon sugar and cream for 20 seconds on medium speed. Scrape the bowl and mix 30 seconds more. Add the eggs, one at a time, and beat well after each addition. Beat in the vanilla. Sift together the flour, baking soda, and salt and add the flour mixture all at once. Mix until the flour is incorporated and stir in the peanuts.

3. Scoop the dough, about ¼ cup for each, onto ungreased baking sheets; there should be no more than nine cookies per sheet. You will need three sheets. Press down lightly with a large fork in two directions to make a cross, flattening the dough slightly. Sprinkle each cookie with ½ teaspoon sugar. Bake for 7 to 9 minutes.

4. Remove from the oven and cool on the baking sheets. The cookies will be very soft, but as they cool they will firm up somewhat, though they will still be soft. Remove the cookies from the sheets when cool and fill with Ganache.

GANACHE

1 pound bittersweet chocolate
1 pint heavy cream

1. Break up the chocolate into small pieces and process in a food processor until it is very fine.

2. Heat the cream to the boiling point. With the food processor on, pour the hot cream through the feed tube and process only until well blended. Remove to another bowl and cool. Refrigerate only long enough so that the Ganache can be spread thickly between two cookies. Spread equally on 12 cookies; top with the remaining cookies.

3. Put in a cool place, covered, for several hours or overnight. The Ganache will seep into the cookies and keep them soft.

HELP NOTE: *The Ganache can also be made ahead and refrigerated tightly covered. It will keep several days. To use, heat the container of Ganache in a bowl of warm water.*
   Not everyone has 3 cookie sheets; just reuse. ❦

SOFT CHOCOLATE
CHIP COOKIES

*E*veryone knows the story of the creation of chocolate chip cookies. I wonder what the creator of this culinary icon would think of today's variations, of the books devoted exclusively to chocolate chip cookies, and of chocolate chip cookie contests.

The essence of chocolate chip cookies is the texture. The proponents of the hard cookies are as vociferous as the proponents of the soft. It's obvious where my sentiments lie.

yield: about 3 dozen large cookies

16 tablespoons (2 sticks) unsalted butter, softened

¾ cup packed dark brown sugar

¾ cup granulated sugar

2 eggs

1 vanilla bean

2¼ cups unbleached all-purpose flour

2 teaspoons powdered instant espresso

1 teaspoon baking soda

½ teaspoon salt

12 ounces bittersweet chocolate, coarsely chopped

1⅓ cups chopped pecans or 2 to 3 tablespoons chocolate nibs (see Help Note, page 149)

1. Place oven racks near the middle of the oven. Preheat the oven to 375 degrees. Grease several baking sheets or line with parchment paper or Silpat mats (see Help Note, page 149).

2. In an electric mixer, cream the butter and sugars, scraping down the sides of the bowl often. Add the eggs, one at a time, beating well after each addition.

3. Cut the vanilla bean in half lengthwise and scrape the seeds into the mixing bowl. Mix well.

4. Sift the flour. Mix the sifted flour with the espresso powder, baking soda, and salt. Slowly beat into the butter mixture until fully incorporated.

5. Mix the chopped chocolate and pecans or nibs into the cookie dough.

6. For large cookies, drop the batter by heaping tablespoonfuls on the cookie sheets. For smaller cookies, drop by heaping teaspoonfuls. For flatter cookies, pat the dough with the back of a spoon before baking. Bake 10 to12 minutes for the larger cookies, 8 to 10 minutes for the smaller cookies. Let the cookies cool slightly on the baking sheets and then remove to racks.

HELP NOTE: *See Sources, page 204, for Silpat mats.*

For crisper cookies, bake a minute or two longer.

I have been making chocolate chip cookies in all of their splendid varieties for fifty years. Today, the biggest difference from the original recipe is the quality of the chocolate. Chocolate that contains more cacao is the key. I am a big fan of Scharffen Berger, which produces a bittersweet chocolate containing 70 percent cacao. The chopped chocolate melts more than the renowned chocolate chips from Nestlé, so the cookies look more chocolatey. Scharffen Berger nibs are roasted, shelled cocoa beans and have a strong, acidic chocolate flavor. Though they are processed with a bit of sugar, they do not taste sweet. They provide a crunch and a flash of chocolatey bitterness. (See Sources, page 203.) ❦

MICHAEL'S
MOCHA BROWNIES

*T*his recipe was originally mine but my son, Michael, improved upon it. The brownies are the deeply chocolate, moist variety that sticks to the roof of your mouth, not too sweet, with a wonderful surprise of bits of finely chopped orange peel throughout. Michael uses Kahlúa, though other coffee-flavored liqueurs can be substituted.

When Michael makes these for his restaurant in Spain, he doubles the recipe. Why don't you? They will never go to waste.

yield: depends entirely on the size of a brownie; for example, 48 to 54 2-inch brownies, depending on the size of the pan

1 pound (4 sticks) unsalted butter	3 cups unbleached all-purpose flour
8 ounces bittersweet chocolate	½ teaspoon salt
8 ounces unsweetened chocolate	¼ cup very finely minced orange peel
3 cups sugar	2 tablespoons coffee extract
10 eggs	5 tablespoons coffee-flavored liqueur

1. Place a rack in the middle of the oven. Preheat the oven to 350 degrees. Grease and flour a 12 by 18-inch baking pan or two 9 by 13-inch baking pans.

2. Melt the butter and chocolates over hot water or in the microwave on medium power. Set aside. In an electric mixer, beat the sugar and eggs thoroughly; stir in the cooled chocolate mixture. Stir in the flour, salt, orange peel, coffee extract, and coffee-flavored liqueur.

3. Spoon the batter into the baking pan(s) and bake the large pan for 20 to 25 minutes, the smaller ones for about 20 minutes. The brownies should be quite moist when tested with a cake tester inserted in the center; some batter should cling to the tester.

4. Cool and cut into squares.

HELP NOTE: The brownies can be refrigerated, or frozen up to a month, well wrapped. It is better not to cut them until they are ready to serve; it keeps them from drying out.

To serve, defrost if frozen or remove from the refrigerator and slice while still cold.

The second day the brownies take on more of the coffee-liqueur flavor. They are between a cake brownie and a fudge brownie with the edges being more cake-like, the center more fudgy.

If you can't find coffee flavoring in your local grocery store or specialty market, see Sources, page 203. ✿

COBBLERS, SHORTCAKES, TARTS, *and* PIES

SUMMER PEACH COBBLER

*J*ust the sound of this name conjures up gingham tablecloths and fried chicken, and a warm summer day in a shady spot.

yield: 12 to 18 servings

FILLING

6 cups peeled fresh ripe peach slices
  (see Help Note, page 153)
1 tablespoon fresh lemon juice
1/3 cup sugar or more, depending on the
  sweetness of the peaches

2 tablespoons unbleached all-purpose flour
1/2 teaspoon ground cinnamon, optional
Batter (see recipe, below)
Topping (see recipe, page 153)

1. Lightly grease a 9 by 13-inch baking pan.

2. Toss the sliced peaches with the lemon juice.

3. Mix together the sugar, flour, and cinnamon, if using. Stir in the peaches and pour into the prepared baking pan. Taste for sweetness and add sugar, if necessary.

BATTER

1 1/2 cups unbleached all-purpose flour
1/3 cup sugar
1/2 teaspoon ground cinnamon
1/4 heaping teaspoon salt
2 1/2 teaspoons baking powder

8 tablespoons (1 stick) unsalted butter,
  cut into small pieces
1 slightly beaten egg
2/3 cup buttermilk
1 teaspoon pure vanilla extract

1. Place a rack in the lower third of the oven. Preheat the oven to 375 degrees.

2. Mix together the flour, sugar, cinnamon, salt, and baking powder.

3. With a pastry blender, cut in pieces of butter until the mixture resembles coarse meal.

4. Whisk together the egg, buttermilk, and vanilla. Pour the wet ingredients into dry and stir to form a soft dough. Do not overmix.

5. Drop the dough by spoonfuls on top of the fruit filling, spacing them evenly. (The dough will not completely cover the fruit.)

TOPPING

2 tablespoons sugar mixed with
 1/4 teaspoon ground cinnamon
 for sprinkling

1. Sprinkle the dough lightly with the sugar-cinnamon mixture.

2. Bake until the topping is golden brown and the filling is bubbling, about 35 to 40 minutes.

3. Serve warm, plain, or with cream or ice cream.

VARIATIONS: *Add 1/4 to 1/2 cup minced crystallized ginger (depending upon how much you like ginger) for ginger peach cobbler. Eliminate the optional cinnamon from the filling.*

Substitute blackberries, blueberries, raspberries, or any combination for all or some of the peaches.

Substitute an equal amount of apricots for the peaches; add currants, if desired.

Substitute an equal amount of apples for the peaches, adding more cinnamon and sugar to the filling.

HELP NOTE: *Blanch the peaches in boiling water for about 15 seconds. Rinse with cold water and the skins should pop right off.* ❦

BLUEBERRY SHORTCAKE WITH BLUEBERRY SAUCE AND LEMON CURD

*J*ust as I was putting the finishing touches to this book, blueberries arrived in full force in Northeastern Vermont, where we spend most summer weekends, and I found I was feeding our frequent weekend guests a lot of blueberry shortcake. This is a modified version of a strawberry-raspberry shortcake that appeared in *The New Elegant but Easy Cookbook*. The question on everyone's lips was: "Is it in your new book?" How could I refuse? One night someone took one small spoonful of chicken salad and one small spoonful of potato salad for dinner in order to have enough room for this not-so-dainty dessert.

yield: 8 servings

BISCUITS

2 cups unbleached all-purpose flour

3 tablespoons brown sugar

1 tablespoon baking powder

¼ teaspoon salt

¼ pound (1 stick) unsalted butter, cut into small pieces, PLUS 16 teaspoons (5 tablespoons PLUS 1 teaspoon) for buttering biscuits, softened

1 teaspoon pure vanilla extract

1 cup heavy cream

Topping and Filling (see recipe, page 155)

Lemon Curd (see recipe, page 155)

Whipped Cream (see recipe, page 156)

1. Place a rack in the middle of the oven and preheat the oven to 425 degrees. Lightly grease a cookie sheet or use a Silpat mat (see Help Note, page 156).

2. In a large bowl, combine the flour, brown sugar, baking powder, and salt. Add the 1 stick butter, cutting it with your fingers until the mixture resembles coarse crumbs. Add the vanilla and cream and mix until the ingredients hold together.

3. Turn the dough out onto a lightly floured board and knead a few times. Press the dough into a rectangle ¾ inch thick. Cut into eight equal pieces.

4. Place the pieces on a cookie sheet and chill for 20 minutes. Bake for 15 to 20 minutes, until the bottoms of the biscuits are browned and the tops are golden. Remove the biscuits and place them on a wire rack to cool. If you are not using the biscuits immediately, wrap them loosely in aluminum foil after they

have cooled and leave at room temperature. The biscuits can be prepared the morning of the day they will be used.

TOPPING AND FILLING

3 pints blueberries, washed and stemmed, room temperature

2 tablespoons orange liqueur or crème de cassis

A little superfine sugar, if needed

1. Mix 1 pint of the berries with the liqueur and stir well. Add the sugar, if needed, and bring the mixture to a boil. Reduce the heat and cook a few minutes until the berries have softened but are not mushy. Cool or chill the mixture overnight in the refrigerator, if desired. Bring to room temperature to serve.

2. Uncooked berries should be at room temperature, too.

LEMON CURD

2 eggs and 1 egg yolk

4 tablespoons (½ stick) unsalted butter, softened

1 cup granulated sugar

Juice of 1½ lemons

Finely grated zest of 1 lemon

1. In a medium heatproof bowl, beat the eggs and yolk until light. Add the butter, sugar, lemon juice, and zest.

2. Place on top of stove over hot water, stirring occasionally, until the mixture begins to thicken. (It should reach 160 degrees on a candy thermometer.)

3. Remove from the heat and cool slightly. Cover with plastic wrap to prevent a crust from forming and refrigerate for up to a week. Leave at room temperature at least 30 minutes before serving.

(continued)

WHIPPED CREAM

    1 cup heavy cream
    2 tablespoons granulated sugar

1. In a large bowl, whip the cream and sugar until medium-soft peaks form. (This may be prepared several hours before serving.)

TO ASSEMBLE

1. Preheat the oven to 400 degrees. Cut the biscuits in half horizontally and spread the cut sides with the 16 teaspoons softened butter. Place the biscuits cut side up on a cookie sheet and heat about 5 minutes.

2. Place the two halves of a biscuit, cut side up, on a dessert plate. Generously spread each half with lemon curd. Top each half with the uncooked blueberries and then with the cooked blueberry sauce. Garnish with the whipped cream.

VARIATION: *Substitute cut-up strawberries for the blueberries.*

HELP NOTE: *Don't be fazed by the length of this recipe. No part of it has to be done at the last minute. The lemon curd will keep a week. The blueberries and sauce can be prepared a day ahead, the biscuits made in the morning, and the cream whipped several hours in advance. Some bakeries make very good biscuits; you might be able to use them instead of making them. Excellent lemon curd is available in jars, but be sure it contains nothing but lemon, sugar, and eggs. No flavorings, colorings, or unpronounceable ingredients should be listed on the label.*

    See Sources, page 204, for Silpat mats. 🌿

LEMON MERINGUE PIE

*S*omewhere in the mid-twentieth century, someone invented a flavoring capsule that was included in the box of My-T-Fine Pudding and Pie Filling. It was used to flavor the filling of a lemon meringue pie and was one of the first convenience foods. But lemon meringue pies made with it were never quite the same as the from-scratch variety, like this version from my mother.

yield: one 10-inch pie, making 8 generous servings or 12 smaller ones

FILLING

1 1/4 cups sugar
1/4 cup cornstarch
1/8 teaspoon salt
6 egg yolks
1/2 cup fresh lemon juice
1 1/2 cups boiling water
3 tablespoons unsalted butter, cut in small
   pieces

Grated rind of 1 large lemon
Roland Mesnier's Anyone-Can-Make Pie
   Crust (see recipe, page 158)
Shrink- and Weep-Proof Meringue (see
   recipe, page 159)

1. Whisk together the sugar, cornstarch, and salt and mix thoroughly.

2. In an electric mixer, beat the yolks until they are pale yellow and thick. Add the sugar mixture and lemon juice and beat well. Gradually beat in the boiling water.

3. Pour the mixture in a pot and bring to a boil, stirring constantly. Immediately lower the heat to a simmer and stir a minute or two until the mixture is very thick. Quickly stir in the butter and grated lemon rind. Remove from the heat and cool; stir occasionally.

4. Pour the cooled filling into the cooled, baked crust. Spoon on the meringue, covering the edges of the crust and making swirl marks with a spoon.

5. Turn on the broiler and place the pie under the broiler to brown the top. (This happens in a matter of seconds so watch very, very carefully.) Remove the pie and cool completely. Cover gently and refrigerate.

(continued)

ROLAND MESNIER'S ANYONE-CAN-MAKE PIE CRUST

Roland has been the pastry chef at the White House since 1980, creating fantasies for state dinners and low-calorie desserts for weight-watching first ladies. He's a very practical man, and after years of making desserts for thousands of people he has perfected simplified methods, including pie crusts that anyone can make.

The pie crusts require very little rolling out and can be made in an electric mixer in 3 minutes. If the pastry tears it can be patched, and it doesn't need to be chilled before rolling. The way Roland decorates pies doesn't require any fancy handiwork to make a pleated crust edge.

yield: 2 crusts

3½ cups cake flour plus more for rolling	½ teaspoon salt
½ cup water	1½ cups shortening
¼ cup sugar	

1. Place a rack in the middle of the oven. Preheat the oven to 375 degrees.

2. Place all the ingredients in a bowl of an electric mixer, and using the paddle attachment of the mixer, mix until well blended, about 3 minutes.

3. Divide the dough in two; shape each into a ball.

4. Place two sheets of wax paper overlapping on a counter and flour the wax paper. Flatten one of the balls with the heel of your hand and press out as much as possible into a round. Flour the rolling pin and roll out the dough to fit a 10-inch pie plate. If the dough breaks, simply patch it with a piece of dough from the edge.

5. Place the pie plate upside down on top of the dough, and using the wax paper, flip over the plate and dough, and carefully fit the dough onto the plate. Remove the wax paper.

6. Using a sharp knife, trim the crust at the edge of the plate. Prick the crust with a fork on the bottom and sides. Crumple a piece of parchment (or wax) paper; open it up and grease one side. Place the paper, grease side down, on the crust to cover the bottom and a little up the sides. Fill the paper with dried beans to keep the crust from puffing.

7. Bake the crust for 5 to 7 minutes, until the edges are browned. Remove the crust from the oven and cover the edges with aluminum foil. Return to the oven

and continue baking for a total of 20 minutes; carefully remove the paper and beans and continue baking 5 to 10 minutes longer, until the rest of the crust is golden. Remove, cool, and fill.

8. Reserve the remaining dough for another pie.

HELP NOTE: *Wrap the remaining dough well and freeze. It will keep at least a month. To use, defrost completely and proceed.*

The pie crust can be made a day ahead, rolled out, wrapped, and held at room temperature before baking.

SHRINK- AND WEEP-PROOF MERINGUE

6 egg whites
10 tablespoons sugar
¼ teaspoon salt

1. Combine the ingredients in a heatproof mixing bowl and place the bowl over a pan of water that is barely simmering. (Water should not touch the bowl.)

2. Stir quickly with a fork while the whites are just barely warm. Test with your finger after 25 seconds; the mixture should feel slightly warm and the sugar should be dissolved. Keep testing every 15 seconds.

3. Remove the meringue from the heat and beat with a handheld mixer at its highest speed until the meringue holds soft peaks. Do not overbeat or it will be hard to spread the meringue.

HELP NOTE: *Bakers have always complained about meringues that weep and pull away from the sides. The trick here is to use a slightly cooked meringue, similar to an Italian meringue. Cooking the egg whites gives the meringue more stability.*

KEY LIME CHIFFON PIE

*N*ot so long ago, most of us could only guess at the taste of a fresh key lime. If we could get anything with the name "key lime" on it, it came in a bottle and had chemicals that made it taste unspeakable.

Now, in season, fresh little key limes are found all over the country, or at the very least, frozen key lime juice, which has no dreadful chemicals.

yield: 6 to 8 servings

GINGERSNAP CRUST

1 1/2 cup gingersnap crumbs
5 1/3 tablespoons (1/3 cup) unsalted butter, melted
2/3 cup crushed pecans

1 teaspoon grated lime peel
Ganache, optional (see recipe, below)
Filling (see recipe, page 161)

1. Place a rack in the middle of the oven. Preheat the oven to 350 degrees.

2. Combine all the ingredients except the Ganache and mix well. Line a 9-inch pie plate with the crumb mixture. Bake 6 to 8 minutes. Remove and cool. If using Ganache, freeze the shell for 30 minutes before lining with the Ganache.

GANACHE (OPTIONAL)

3 ounces bittersweet chocolate, broken into small pieces
6 tablespoons heavy cream

1. Place the chocolate in a bowl. In a saucepan, bring the cream to a boil. Pour the cream over the chocolate and let sit for 3 minutes.

2. Starting in the center of the bowl, whisk well to combine. Cool to a warm temperature and pour on top of the frozen crust. The Ganache will set almost immediately. If there is any Ganache left, use it to decorate the filling.

FILLING

1 package unflavored gelatin	¼ cup water
1 cup sugar	2 teaspoons grated lime peel
¼ teaspoon salt	1½ cups heavy cream
4 eggs, separated	6 to 8 very thin slices lime for garnish
½ cup key lime juice	

1. In a saucepan, mix the gelatin with ½ cup of the sugar and the salt. Thoroughly beat the egg yolks together with the lime juice and water and stir into the gelatin mixture.

2. Cook over medium heat, stirring, just until the mixture comes to a boil. Remove from the heat and stir in 1 teaspoon lime peel. Chill, stirring occasionally, until the mixture mounds lightly when dropped from a spoon.

3. Beat the egg whites until soft peaks form. Gradually beat in the remaining ½ cup sugar. Fold into the gelatin mixture.

4. Whip 1 cup of the cream and fold into the filling. Spoon the filling into the shell and chill until firm. Whip the remaining cream and top the pie with mounds of it. Decorate the mounds with thin slices of lime and the remaining grated rind, and drizzle any leftover Ganache, if using, over the filling.

HELP NOTE: *If all else fails, use Persian limes (which are larger and greener than key limes). Under no circumstances use bottled key lime juice. It will strip off paint.*

Check the sweetness of the gingersnaps and nuts together before adding any sugar. It may not need additional sugar.

Sometimes it is difficult to cut a crumb crust without making a mess. An easy way is to line a pie pan with foil, press in the crust, bake, and freeze. When frozen, gently remove the crust, still in the foil, from the pan, and then peel the foil from the crust. Put the frozen crust back in the pie pan and proceed.

If you don't like gingersnaps you can use a standard graham cracker crust.

"Ganache" is a French term for a combination of chocolate and cream. It makes a fine frosting or filling and may be one of the easiest things to make. 🌿

MOM'S APPLE PIE

I liked my mother's apple pie, but Sue Simon's mother's apple pie has all the little tricks that make it fabulous instead of merely wonderful.

yield: one 11-inch pie to serve 10 to 12 people

APPLE FILLING

5 pounds Granny Smith apples
1 cup sugar, PLUS sugar for sprinkling on
   unbaked crust
3 tablespoons flour
3½ teaspoons ground cinnamon
1 teaspoon lemon juice

2 tablespoons milk, PLUS additional milk
   for brushing the unbaked crust
2 tablespoons unsalted butter, cut in small
   cubes
Double-Crust Flaky Pastry (see recipe,
   page 163)

1. Peel, core, and slice the apples ¾ inch thick.

2. Place a rack in the middle of the oven. Preheat the oven to 425 degrees. Combine the 1 cup sugar, flour, and cinnamon. Sprinkle the bottom crust with some of this mixture.

3. Add a single layer of apples. Sprinkle with more of the cinnamon mixture and continue layering in this fashion until the apples and cinnamon mixture are gone.

4. Sprinkle the apples with the lemon juice, 2 tablespoons milk, and the butter cubes.

5. Cover the apples with the top crust and crimp the edges. Cut a few vents in the top crust with a small knife. Brush the top crust with a little milk and lightly sprinkle with sugar.

6. Bake the pie at 425 degrees for 10 minutes. Lower the heat to 350 degrees and bake about 40 to 45 minutes longer, or until the top crust is browned and the bottom crust looks baked and the apples are tender but not mushy when pierced with a cake tester.

DOUBLE-CRUST FLAKY PASTRY

2½ cups unbleached all-purpose flour
1 tablespoon sugar
1 teaspoon salt
16 tablespoons (2 sticks) very cold
   unsalted butter, cut in small pieces

1 tablespoon cider vinegar
¼ to ⅜ cup ice water
Flour for rolling

1. Stir together the dry ingredients and chill about 1 hour. (This can be done in the food processor or by hand.) Cut in the butter with a pastry blender or two forks or pulse until the mixture resembles coarse meal.

2. Add the vinegar and ice water, 1 tablespoon at a time, stirring with a fork (or pulsing a few times in the processor) until the mixture barely holds together when pinched between two fingers. Do not add any more water than necessary and do not overprocess.

3. Divide the dough into two unequal parts (one half of the dough should be slightly larger than the other) and place each on a sheet of plastic wrap. Gather up the ends of the plastic wrap, twist closed, then flatten each piece of dough into a disk, and chill for 30 minutes.

4. Remove the smaller piece of dough from the refrigerator. Let stand a few minutes. Roll the smaller piece of dough into a circle on a lightly floured board with a floured rolling pin, always rolling from the center outward. The dough should be less than ⅛ inch thick. Line the bottom of an 11-inch pie plate with dough and chill while rolling out the larger piece of dough, which will become the top crust.

HELP NOTE: You can use shortening or lard in the pie crust.

If crimping the edges of a pie crust makes you shudder, refer back to Roland Mesnier's crust recipe (page 158) and simply seal the bottom and top crusts and use the little kitchen gadget called a crimper that makes the edge look crimped. ❦

CARAMEL APPLE TART

*W*hen you want the taste of apple pie but don't want to go through the trouble of making a crust, this is a sumptuous alternative. It's oozing with caramelized apples, sugar, and butter.

yield: 6 servings

10 sheets phyllo (see Help Note, page 165)
8 tablespoons (1 stick) unsalted butter
¾ cup sugar
Grated rind of 1 orange
1 tablespoon lemon juice
¼ teaspoon ground cardamom
2 tablespoons brandy

1¾ pounds small apples, peeled, cored, and quartered (4 or 5 apples)
8 tablespoons (1 stick) melted butter for brushing phyllo
Whipped cream or vanilla ice cream as accompaniment

1. Open the package of phyllo and cover with a damp cloth. Place a stack of 10 sheets of phyllo on a work surface. Trace a 12-inch circle on the phyllo pile and cut through all the sheets of the phyllo to create 10 circles. Cover with a damp cloth and refrigerate. Wrap the remaining phyllo in an airtight bag and use on another occasion. Phyllo will last about a week.

2. Place a rack in the middle of the oven. Preheat the oven to 425 degrees.

3. Melt the butter in a skillet that is 12 inches at the top and about 9 inches on the bottom. Remove from heat and stir in the sugar, orange rind, lemon juice, cardamom, and brandy until the sugar is dissolved. Arrange the apple quarters, tightly packed, on the sugar in concentric circles. Place the pan over medium-high heat and bring to a simmer; cook until the butter-sugar mixture takes on a golden color and the apples are soft, 20 to 50 minutes, depending on the size of the apple quarters. Baste the apples occasionally with the syrup. Watch carefully so it doesn't burn.

4. Remove from the heat. Remove the phyllo from the refrigerator and keep it covered with a damp cloth. Brush one sheet of phyllo with melted butter; place it on top of the apples, buttered side up. Repeat until all the phyllo is used. Then cut a ½-inch hole in the middle of the phyllo to let the steam escape.

5. Carefully tuck the overlapping edges of the phyllo into the sides of the pan and bake until the phyllo is browned, 10 to 15 minutes.

6. Remove the pan from the oven and cool for 10 minutes. Run a sharp knife along the sides to separate the tart from the pan. Place a serving tray on top of the pan and flip so that the phyllo is at the bottom, apples on top. Cut while still warm.

7. Serve with whipped cream or vanilla ice cream.

HELP NOTE: *Phyllo are the paper-thin sheets of pastry used for so many Greek pastries like baklava. Many supermarkets carry them in the frozen food case. Fresh is better, but not so easily available unless there is a Greek market near you. Completely defrost frozen phyllo in the refrigerator or at room temperature before using.*

If you want to serve the dish a few hours after making, do not flip the tart until just before serving so that the phyllo does not get soggy. Reheat at 350 degrees to warm through. ❦

APPLE ALMOND CRISP

The British call crisps "crumbles." Whatever the name, they are an easy alternative to pies, with no crust to make but all the fruit flavor with a topping of butter, sugar, and flour.

yield: 6 to 8 servings

APPLES
7 to 8 cups firm, peeled, cored
    tart-sweet apples, cut in 1-inch
    chunks
3 to 5 tablespoons lemon juice
¼ to ½ cup sugar
¼ cup maple syrup
1 tablespoon grated lemon rind
1 teaspoon ground cinnamon
½ teaspoon ground nutmeg
Few shakes salt to taste
Topping (see below)

TOPPING
½ cup sugar
¾ cup unbleached all-purpose flour
½ teaspoon ground cinnamon
½ teaspoon salt
8 tablespoons (1 stick) cold unsalted
    butter, cut in ½-inch pieces
1 cup sliced almonds

Vanilla ice cream, whipped cream, or
    Crème Fraîche (see recipe, page 167)
    as an accompaniment

1. Place a rack in the bottom third of the oven. Preheat the oven to 375 degrees.

2. Grease a 2-quart ovenproof glass or earthenware casserole that is at least 2 inches deep.

3. Mix the apples with the lemon juice, sugar, maple syrup, lemon rind, cinnamon, nutmeg, and salt. (The amount of lemon juice and sugar you use will depend on the flavor of the apples, so taste them.) Place the apples in the casserole.

4. To make the topping, stir the sugar, flour, cinnamon, and salt together. Add the butter and in a mixer or a food processor, mix together only until crumbly. Stir in the almonds.

5. Cover evenly with the topping and bake for 50 to 60 minutes until the juices are bubbling and the top has browned. In most ovens it is a good idea to turn the dish once or twice to brown evenly, because the back of the oven is usually hotter than the front.

6. Cool at least 10 minutes before serving. Serve warm or at room temperature with vanilla ice cream, whipped cream, or Crème Fraîche (page 167).

VARIATIONS: Replace the apples with an equal amount of blueberries or peaches. If you use peaches, add 1/2 teaspoon ground nutmeg.

HELP NOTE: I use maple syrup instead of honey in the filling because I prefer it, but you could use honey instead, or you could add additional sugar. Maple syrup adds its own flavor; sugar adds only sweetness.

The Brits use oatmeal instead of flour in their toppings, and you can, too.

You can make the topping 3 days ahead and refrigerate it if you want to cut down on last-minute work.

If there are leftovers they can be reheated in a 300-degree oven. ❦

CRÈME FRAÎCHE

No, Crème Fraîche was not a comfort food of my childhood. But it is now. If you can't find Crème Fraîche, you can make it yourself quite easily.

yield: 1 pint

> 2 cups heavy cream
> 2 tablespoons buttermilk

1. Pour the cream into a container with a top. Stir in the buttermilk. Cover loosely and leave in a warm place, such as the back of a gas stove, until the cream thickens to the consistency of whole-milk yogurt. This can take as little as overnight or as long as a day.

2. Store in the refrigerator for up to 2 weeks.

HELP NOTE: Do not use ultrapasteurized cream. The better the cream, the better the Crème Fraîche. Some organic creams are so rich in butterfat the cream practically whips itself. ❦

CAKES

WILMA HEAD'S SOUR CREAM POUND CAKE

*W*hen pound cakes appeared in the late nineteenth and early twentieth centuries, they were aptly named, as they contained a pound of each ingredient. Today we find that recipe too dry.

After I made several attempts to find a dense, buttery pound cake that was not dry, Tom Head, a Southerner and executive food editor and restaurant reviewer of *The Washingtonian* magazine, came to the rescue, providing me with his mother's recipe.

Wilma Head's pound cake is moist and dense with a crackling crust. And it's big, requiring a 10-inch tube pan.

yield: one 10-inch tube cake, serving 12 to 14

16 tablespoons (2 sticks) unsalted butter, softened	½ teaspoon salt
	¼ teaspoon baking soda
3 cups sugar	8 ounces sour cream
6 eggs, separated	1 teaspoon pure vanilla extract
3 cups sifted unbleached all-purpose flour	1 teaspoon pure almond extract

1. Place a rack in the middle of the oven. Preheat oven to 300 degrees. Butter and flour a 10-inch tube or bundt pan. Cut out a piece of wax paper to fit the bottom and place on the bottom of the pan.

2. Cream the butter and sugar in a mixer until thoroughly blended.

3. Beat the egg yolks separately and then beat into the butter mixture.

4. Combine the sifted flour, salt, and baking soda. Sift together two more times. Alternately beat the flour mixture and the sour cream into the butter mixture with the extracts.

5. Beat the egg whites until stiff but not dry. Stir one-third of the whites into the batter and fold in the remaining whites. Spoon the batter into the prepared tube pan and bake about 1½ hours, until a cake tester inserted in the center comes out clean.

6. Remove the pan from the oven and cool for 5 minutes on a wire rack. With a knife, separate the sides of the cake from the pan and from the tube. Remove the cake from pan and cool completely.

VARIATIONS: *Ginger pound cake: Omit the vanilla and almond extracts and add 1½ table-spoons ground ginger.*

You could also replace the almond extract with 2 tablespoons of rum, brandy, or orange juice.

For a traditional New England pound cake, omit the vanilla and almond extracts and add 1½ teaspoons ground mace.

Try a slice toasted, spread with unsalted butter.

HELP NOTE: *Pound cakes keep well, wrapped and refrigerated, or frozen for a month. In fact, this cake is better after it has rested a day or two.* ❦

GINGERED GINGERBREAD WITH GINGER ICE CREAM

With a bow to the divine Marion Cunningham, author of *The Fannie Farmer Cookbook* (Knopf, 1996) and many other cookbooks, cooking teacher, and kind, generous friend.

*B*efore gingerbread became a dessert, it was served as a bread.

yield: 9 squares

2½ cups unbleached all-purpose flour
1 teaspoon ground cinnamon
1 teaspoon powdered ginger
¼ teaspoon ground cloves
8 tablespoons (1 stick) unsalted butter, softened
½ cup sugar

1 cup dark molasses
2 teaspoons baking soda
1 cup boiling water
2 lightly beaten eggs
3 tablespoons chopped crystallized ginger
1 pint ginger ice cream (see Help Note, page 171)

1. Place a rack in the lower third of the oven. Preheat the oven to 350 degrees. Grease and flour an 8-inch square metal baking pan and line the bottom with wax paper.

2. Combine the flour, cinnamon, ginger, and cloves and sift together.

3. Beat the butter in an electric mixer until creamy. Add the sugar and molasses and beat until well blended.

4. Stir the baking soda into the boiling water and beat into butter-sugar mixture.

5. Slowly beat in the dry ingredients until smooth; beat in the eggs. Stir in the crystallized ginger.

6. Pour into the prepared pan and bake for 35 to 45 minutes or until a cake tester or toothpick inserted in the center comes out clean.

7. Remove the pan from the oven and cool for 10 minutes on a wire rack. Turn the gingerbread out onto a rack and cool.

8. Serve warm or cool (warm is best) cut into squares, topped with ginger ice cream.

HELP NOTE: *This cake can be made a day ahead, covered with foil, and stored at room temperature. To serve, wrap in foil and heat 10 minutes or so in a 350-degree oven. Cut before serving.*

Adding cut-up crystallized ginger intensifies the ginger flavor of the cake. For a good darker version of the cake, use blackstrap molasses.

If you cannot find ginger ice cream, make your own by softening a pint of good vanilla ice cream and stirring in 4 tablespoons of finely chopped crystallized ginger. Freeze again until ready to use. One of the best ginger ice creams I have ever eaten is from Reed's; it seems to make its way mostly to natural food stores (see Sources, page 204). 🌿

DIONE LUCAS' CHOCOLATE ROLL

Dione Lucas was a cooking teacher, probably the first on television, in the 1950s. I learned this incredible dessert in classes I took with her.

When she taught before a large group she loved to sample whatever alcohol was to be used in cooking—directly from the bottle—more than once. She was a great showman and a great teacher.

Described in the original *Elegant but Easy Cookbook* (1960) as "Marian's favorite dessert," it has lost none of its luster. Not a thing has been changed, though today it is possible to buy much better quality chocolate. Use the best you can find (see Sources, page 203).

Here's my disaster story: I had made a chocolate roll the morning of a party, and when I started to roll it up, it collapsed into a dozen sections, the whipped cream oozing out. I spooned it into a pretty glass bowl and served it as chocolate whipped cream pudding. The taste was great; the appearance left something to be desired. The guests inhaled it, none the wiser.

yield: 8 to 10 servings

7 eggs, separated	Pinch salt
1 cup sugar	2 cups heavy cream
½ pound bittersweet chocolate	2 tablespoons rum
7 tablespoons brewed coffee	Unsweetened cocoa for sprinkling

1. Place a rack in the lower third of the oven. Preheat the oven to 350 degrees. Oil a 10 by 15-inch jelly roll pan. Cover with buttered wax paper.

2. In a small mixing bowl, beat the egg yolks and sugar until they are light, fluffy, and creamy. Melt the chocolate with the coffee over very low heat; cool slightly. Meanwhile, beat the egg whites with the salt until stiff but not dry. Mix the yolks with the chocolate and then fold in the whites.

3. Spoon the mixture into the prepared pan and spread to level the top. Bake 15 to 20 minutes in a gas oven or 12 minutes in an electric oven. Remove the pan and cool for 5 minutes. Cover with a slightly damp cloth and cool completely to room temperature.

4. Refrigerate, covered, for 1 hour. Whip the cream and fold in the rum. Remove the cloth carefully from the roll and sprinkle the top generously with the cocoa. Arrange two sheets of wax paper so they overlap. Turn the cake out onto the wax paper and carefully remove the wax paper that lined the pan.

5. Spread the whipped cream over the cake and carefully roll up from the long side, using the wax paper to help with the rolling; roll the cake directly onto a chocolate roll board if you have one or a long, flat serving plate.

6. This cake cracks as it rolls: it should resemble the bark of a tree.

7. Refrigerate.

8. To serve, slice.

HELP NOTE: *This is a very delicate cake, and the directions must be followed to the letter or it won't be possible to roll it up.*

The roll may be prepared 1 day ahead, wrapped well, and refrigerated. 🌿

PINEAPPLE UPSIDE-DOWN CAKE

*G*one are the canned pineapple slices of yesteryear. Fresh pineapple gives a delightful acidity to the sweet cake, which has a creamy texture. The buttermilk makes the tenderest cake base I have ever had for this old favorite.

yield: 8 servings

4 tablespoons (½ stick) PLUS
  8 tablespoons (1 stick) unsalted butter
¾ cup packed dark brown sugar
1 ripe small pineapple, trimmed, quartered,
  cored, and cut in ¼-inch-thick slices (or
  the equivalent number of pieces from
  already cut-up pineapple, 5 or 6 slices)
1 cup granulated sugar

2 eggs
2 cups sifted cake flour
1 teaspoon baking powder
½ teaspoon baking soda
½ teaspoon salt
¾ cup plus 2 tablespoons buttermilk
1 teaspoon pure vanilla extract

1. Place a rack in the bottom third of the oven. Preheat the oven to 350 degrees. Butter the sides of a 9-inch springform pan.

2. Melt the 4 tablespoons butter in a small pan and stir in the brown sugar over medium heat. Cook the mixture, stirring constantly, until the sugar is melted and the mixture is smooth. Immediately pour into the prepared pan and spread to coat the bottom evenly. Place the pineapple slices in a decorative pattern on top of the brown sugar mixture and press lightly. Set aside.

3. In an electric mixer, cream the remaining stick of butter until it is light. Gradually add the granulated sugar and continue beating until the mixture is light. Scrape down the sides of the bowl often.

4. Beat in the eggs.

5. Sift the sifted flour with the baking powder, baking soda, and salt. Add alternately to the creamed mixture with the buttermilk and vanilla, using a mixer set at low speed. Scrape down the sides often. Spoon the batter over the fruit and spread evenly.

6. Bake 40 to 45 minutes. The cake is done if it springs back when pressed lightly in the center. Or use a cake tester, and when it comes out clean the cake is done.

7. Immediately run a knife around the edges. Place a flat plate on the pan and quickly invert. Allow to sit for 5 minutes and then carefully remove the pan and serve the cake warm or at room temperature.

HELP NOTE: *You can make this in the morning and serve it at night. Don't refrigerate before serving. If you want to keep it longer—it will last 2 or 3 days—refrigerate it. Return to room temperature before serving.*

This is a very moist, fine-textured cake. It was originally made in an iron skillet, and if you have one, use it, but a deep 9-inch pan works just as well. Just be sure it is deep enough.

It is not written in stone that an upside-down cake must be made with pineapple. You can use apricots, peaches, sweet cherries, or a mixture of fruit.

Susan Simon, who helped with the recipe testing for this book, said her family always serves pineapple upside-down cake with Chantilly cream. Why not!

To make Chantilly cream, beat heavy cream to a mousse-like consistency and sweeten with superfine granulated sugar and a little vanilla. 🌾

COCONUT CAKE

I must have looked at twenty recipes for coconut cakes. They ranged from those that had coconut only in the frosting (most of them) to one that had coconut milk poured into holes made in the cake layers (sounded pretty soggy).

My version is a happy medium: Lots of coconut flavor throughout and moist but not soggy.

yield: 1 large four-layer nine-inch cake, serving 10 to 12

CAKE

1¾ cups grated fresh unsweetened coconut

1 cup scalded coconut milk, PLUS 1 cup coconut milk

16 tablespoons (2 sticks) unsalted butter, softened

1½ cups sugar

3 eggs

1 teaspoon pure vanilla extract

3 cups sifted cake flour

4 teaspoons baking powder

1 teaspoon salt

Seven-Minute Coconut Frosting (see recipe, page 177)

1. Place a rack in the lower third of the oven. Preheat the oven to 350 degrees. Cut two pieces of wax paper to fit into the bottoms of two 9-inch cake pans. Butter and flour the sides of the pans.

2. Place the coconut in the scalded coconut milk and allow to cool while making the cake.

3. In an electric mixer, cream the butter until it is light; add the sugar and continue beating until light.

4. Add the eggs, one at a time, beating well after each addition. Beat in the vanilla.

5. Sift the flour, baking powder, and salt together and add alternately to the butter-sugar mixture with the remaining cup of coconut milk

6. Press the coconut into a strainer to remove the excess milk. Stir 1 cup of the coconut into the batter and spoon the batter evenly into the two pans. Reserve the remaining coconut for the frosting.

7. Bake 20 to 30 minutes, switching the pans front to back after 15 minutes. The cakes are done when a tester inserted in the center comes out clean.

8. Remove the pans from the oven and place on wire racks to cool for 10 minutes. Run a knife around the edge of the layers and turn out the cakes onto racks to cool completely.

9. To fill and frost: cut each layer in half through the middle to make four layers. Place one layer on a serving plate; generously spread the frosting on top. Top with second layer; repeat. Top with third layer; repeat. Top with a fourth layer and frost the top and sides of the cake.

10. Refrigerate, covered, for several hours; return to room temperature an hour before serving time. Serve in small slices.

SEVEN-MINUTE COCONUT FROSTING

I egg white	I teaspoon pure vanilla extract
¾ cup sugar	¾ cup steeped coconut
⅛ teaspoon salt	(from cake recipe)
⅓ cup light corn syrup	

1. In the top of a double boiler over simmering water, using a handheld electric beater, beat the egg white, sugar, salt, and corn syrup for about 7 minutes or until soft peaks form.

2. Remove from the water and stir in the vanilla. Continue to beat until the frosting is stiff enough to spread over the cake. Stir in the coconut.

HELP NOTE: *If you don't have a cake cover, place toothpicks in the top of the cake and carefully wrap foil around the cake, keeping the foil away from the frosting.*

Most recipes call for a two-layer cake but with four layers you get more frosting and filling.

The first frosting I learned to make was Seven-Minute Frosting. I have seen recipes that would send the novice running to the store for canned frosting. They warn that the temperature of the simmering water has to be exact—not hotter than a certain number of degrees and not cooler. Not true. This frosting is very forgiving and, as it says, it takes only 7 minutes.

Today it's much easier to make a coconut cake; you don't have to grate the coconut yourself. Thanks to the popularity of Thai cooking in this country, you can buy fresh or frozen unsweetened grated coconut and canned unsweetened coconut milk. Just be sure to read the label on the can. You want coconut milk, not cream. ❧

CARROT CAKE WITH CREAM CHEESE FROSTING

*T*his is a cake from the 1950s that has become as ubiquitous as chocolate chip cookies.

This version calls for canned crushed pineapple. I've tried it with and without; I'm voting for crushed pineapple because of the moisture it adds to the cake.

I've seen many different frostings used on carrot cake, but I opt only for the cream cheese version because it provides just the right contrast to the texture of the cake.

yield: one 9-inch layer cake, serving 10 to 12,
or two 8-inch loaf cakes, serving 16
(see Help Note, page 179)

CAKE

1½ cups unbleached all-purpose
  flour
½ cup packed brown sugar
¾ cup granulated sugar
1 teaspoon baking powder
1 teaspoon baking soda
½ teaspoon salt
1 teaspoon ground cinnamon
½ teaspoon ground nutmeg
½ teaspoon ground cloves

½ teaspoon allspice
¾ cup vegetable oil
3 eggs
1½ cups finely grated raw carrots
½ cup thoroughly drained canned
  crushed pineapple
1 cup raisins
1 cup finely chopped walnuts
Cream Cheese Frosting (see recipe,
  page 179)

1. Place a rack in the lower third of the oven. Preheat the oven to 350 degrees. Grease and flour two 9-inch round cake tins or two 8½ by 4½-inch loaf pans. Place a piece of wax paper, cut to size, on the bottom of each pan.

2. In an electric mixer, stir the flour, sugars, baking powder, baking soda, salt, and spices until they are well blended.

3. Beat in the oil at medium speed until it is blended. Add the eggs and continue beating until the batter is smooth.

4. Stir in the carrots, pineapple, raisins, and walnuts.

5. Spoon the batter equally into each pan and bake 35 to 45 minutes until a cake tester inserted in the center comes out clean. Remove the pans from the oven

and place them on racks to cool for 5 minutes. Turn the cakes out onto the racks, remove the wax paper, and cool right side up.

6. When cool, fill and frost the 9-inch layers. Frost the tops of the 8-inch loaf cakes.

CREAM CHEESE FROSTING

4 tablespoons (½ stick) unsalted butter, at room temperature
8 ounces cream cheese, at room temperature

2 cups confectioners' sugar
1 teaspoon pure vanilla extract
2 teaspoons orange extract
1 tablespoon grated orange rind

1. Beat the butter until it is smooth and creamy. Beat in the cream cheese, sugar, vanilla, and orange extract until smooth.

2. Stir in the orange rind.

3. Be careful not to overbeat or the cream cheese could break down. If the frosting is too stiff to spread, beat a few seconds longer.

HELP NOTE: *The cake is best if refrigerated overnight to meld the flavors. The cakes can be frozen without the frosting, well wrapped, up to a month.*

You will have more than enough frosting for the loaf cakes.

It seems strange that even though the amount of batter is the same, baking it in a round pan will provide fewer servings than baking it in a loaf pan; obviously the size of the serving will be different but you can always adjust it. 🌿

TRIPLE GINGER CHEESECAKE

*C*heesecake and ginger are the perfect companions: The richness of the cake is brightened and lightened with ginger four ways. It appeals even to those who say they couldn't possibly eat such a heavy dessert.

yield: 12 to 16 servings

CRUST

Melted butter for brushing
2 cups toasted ground pecans
2 tablespoons dark brown sugar
1 egg white, beaten until frothy

1 teaspoon powdered ginger
1 teaspoon finely grated lemon rind
Filling (see recipe, below)

1. Cut a 9-inch parchment or wax paper circle to fit the bottom of a 9-inch springform pan. Generously brush the bottom and sides of the pan with melted butter, line with the parchment circle, and butter the parchment.

2. Move the oven racks to the bottom of the oven. Preheat the oven to 300 degrees. Prepare a water bath in a shallow pan to sit on the bottom rack. (A jelly roll pan or a 9 by 13-inch baking pan works well.) The pan you have prepared for the cheesecake will bake on the higher rack, rather than directly in the water.

3. Mix the pecans with the brown sugar, egg white, ginger, and lemon rind, just until the mixture is bound together. Press into the bottom and sides of the prepared springform pan.

FILLING

2 pounds cream cheese, room
    temperature
1½ cups sugar
½ cup heavy cream
One 8-ounce jar ginger marmalade or
    preserves, or one 8.5-ounce jar
    crystallized ginger puree

4 eggs PLUS 1 egg yolk
1 teaspoon pure vanilla extract
2 teaspoons powdered ginger
1 tablespoon finely grated fresh gingerroot

Minced crystallized ginger for garnish

1. In an electric mixer, beat the cream cheese until absolutely smooth. Add the granulated sugar and beat until light and fluffy. Add the cream. Add the ginger marmalade or puree and mix well.

2. Add the eggs and egg yolk, one at a time, beating well after each addition. Add the vanilla, powdered ginger, and fresh gingerroot. Mix well. Pour onto the prepared nut crust.

3. Bake at 300 degrees for about 1 hour and 40 minutes. The edges of the cake will be firm, but the center will be soft. Turn off the oven, and cool the cake in the oven for 1 hour. Cool completely before chilling in the refrigerator for at least 4 hours or overnight.

4. Decorate with crystallized ginger.

HELP NOTE: *The ginger products are sometimes available in the ordinary supermarket or you can order them on-line (see Sources, page 203). At this writing they are expected to be available through Williams-Sonoma under their private label.*

BLACK-AND-WHITE CHEESECAKE

A marbleized cheesecake is one of the prettiest, and the slight bitterness and acidity of the chocolate provide a delightful counterpoint to the richness of the white part. The chocolate and almond crust is just the icing on the cake, so to speak.

yield: 12 to 16 servings

CRUST

Melted butter to grease paper	1 cup chopped toasted almonds
4 ounces semisweet chocolate	¼ teaspoon pure almond extract
3 tablespoons unsalted butter	Filling (see recipe, page 183)

1. Cut a 9-inch parchment or wax paper circle to fit the bottom of a 9-inch springform pan. Generously brush the bottom and sides of the pan with melted butter, line with the parchment circle, and butter the parchment. Wrap the outside of the pan with heavy-duty foil, as it will be placed in a water bath. (You don't want to take the chance that your springform will leak.)

2. Move the oven rack to the bottom third of the oven. Preheat the oven to 350 degrees.

3. Prepare a water bath for the cheesecake pan to sit in. (The pan you use for the bath must not be taller than 3 inches.)

4. Melt the chocolate over hot water. Stir in the butter, almonds, and extract. Chill until thick enough to spread over the bottom and sides of the prepared pan, then chill again.

FILLING

6 ounces semisweet or bittersweet
    chocolate, broken into very small pieces
1/4 cup heavy cream
1 1/2 pounds cream cheese, room
    temperature

1 1/2 cups sugar
3 eggs
2 cups sour cream
1 teaspoon pure vanilla extract
Shaved chocolate for decoration, optional

1. Melt the chocolate in the heavy cream over hot water, stirring until smooth. Set aside to cool.

2. In an electric mixer, beat the cream cheese until absolutely smooth. Add the sugar and beat until light and fluffy.

3. Add the eggs, one at a time, beating well after each addition. Add the sour cream and vanilla and mix well.

4. Combine the chocolate mixture with about 2 cups of the cheesecake batter. The resulting chocolate batter must be pourable. If it is too thick to pour, add a little more cheesecake batter.

5. Spoon half of the plain batter into the prepared springform pan. Add spoonfuls of half the chocolate batter, taking care that some of the chocolate batter actually touches the edges of the pan. This will make for a prettier cake. Add the remaining plain batter and then spoonfuls of the remaining chocolate batter. With a knife, draw lines through the chocolate batter into the plain batter to marbleize.

6. Place the pan in the water bath and bake for 70 to 80 minutes. The cake will be golden, firm at the edges but still soft in the center. Cool, then chill for several hours or overnight.

HELP NOTE: The cocoa butter content differs drastically with different brands of chocolate. Rich, dark chocolate like Scharffen Berger or Valrhona will result in a much thicker chocolate batter than Nestlé brand, so you may need to add a little more vanilla batter to thin it.

    For those who cannot eat nuts, a graham cracker crust can always be substituted. ❦

PLUM TORTE

*B*ecause of reader demand, this recipe was published in one form or another in *The New York Times* almost every year between 1983 and 1995, when the then editor of the food section told me to tell my readers it was the last year it would be published, and if they lost it, it was too bad. She suggested they cut it out, laminate it, and put it on the refrigerator door.

My coauthor of the first *Elegant but Easy Cookbook* brought this recipe to the book. Its appeal comes from its lovely old-fashioned flavor and its speed of preparation. It was originally called Fruit Torte.

yield: 8 servings

¾ cup PLUS 1 or 2 tablespoons sugar
8 tablespoons (1 stick) unsalted butter
1 cup unbleached all-purpose flour, sifted
1 teaspoon baking powder
2 eggs

Pinch salt
24 halves pitted Italian (aka prune or purple) plums
1 teaspoon ground cinnamon, or more
Vanilla ice cream, optional

1. Arrange a rack in the lower third of the oven. Preheat the oven to 350 degrees.

2. In an electric mixer, cream the ¾ cup sugar and butter. Add the flour, baking powder, eggs, and salt and beat to mix well. Place in a 9- or 10-inch ungreased springform pan. Cover the top with the plums, skin side down. Mix the cinnamon with the remaining 1 or 2 tablespoons of sugar and sprinkle over the top.

3. Bake for 40 to 50 minutes, until the center tests done with a toothpick. Remove and cool to room temperature or serve warm. Serve plain or with vanilla ice cream.

HELP NOTE: *The torte may be refrigerated or frozen for several months, well wrapped. To serve, return to room temperature and reheat at 300 degrees until warm.* 🌿

REFRIGERATOR DESSERTS

APRICOT MOUSSE

*M*ousses are delightfully cooling and refreshing desserts, perfect for a summer meal.

yield: 6 to 8 servings

2 cups dried apricots

2 cups orange juice

4 tablespoons or more sugar, depending on tartness of fruit, PLUS 4 tablespoons sugar for the egg whites

1 envelope unflavored gelatin

1/4 cup water

1/2 cup lemon juice, approximately

1 tablespoon finely grated lemon rind

2 teaspoons finely grated orange rind

4 tablespoons Grand Marnier

1 teaspoon apricot essence (see Help Note, page 186)

Dash salt

3 egg whites

1 1/2 cups heavy cream

1. Simmer the apricots in the orange juice in a covered pot until tender. Stir in 4 tablespoons or more of sugar.

2. Soften the gelatin in 1/4 cup cold water. Set aside.

3. Drain the apricots and reserve the orange juice, and process apricots to a puree with the lemon juice and lemon and orange rinds in a food processor, using as much lemon as needed to make a tart-sweet mixture.

4. Combine the puree with the softened gelatin and 1/2 cup of the orange juice used for cooking, and cook over low heat to melt the gelatin completely. Remove from the heat and stir in the Grand Marnier, apricot essence, and salt. Set aside.

5. Whip the egg whites until foamy. Gradually beat in the 4 tablespoons sugar and beat until the whites are stiff. Fold the mixture into the puree.

6. Beat 1 cup of the heavy cream to form soft peaks and fold into the puree mixture. Spoon the mousse into individual parfait glasses, coupes, or wineglasses.

(continued)

Cover each glass with wax paper or plastic wrap and refrigerate for a few hours or overnight.

7. To serve, whip the remaining heavy cream and top each glass with some.

HELP NOTE: *Apricot essence is available at many specialty food shops, or see Sources, page 203.* ❦

TERRINE OF SUMMER FRUIT

*T*his is my nod to the Jell-O molds of my childhood as well as to the days when I was a young hostess and served a layered gelatin salad at every important meal! Lately I've no⁺ elaborate layered versions of these in a number of New York City restaurants.

A couple of summers ago I made this at our house in Vermont when the ᴴ their prime. Very light, very refreshing, it requires the ripest fruit as well a. sweet dessert wine. Our weekend guests, especially the women, kept asking foɪ

yield: 8 ⸱⸱⸱ gs

3 cups small strawberries
2 cups raspberries
3 cups total mixed blackberries and
blueberries
2 cups sweet dessert wine like Muscat de
Beaumes de Venise or late-harvest
Riesling

¼ cup superfine sugar
2 envelopes unflavored gelatin
1 tablespoon lime juice
Whipped cream for topping, or whipped
cream–yogurt topping (see Help Note,
page 188), optional

1. Wash and dry the fruit. Trim the stems from the strawberries; set aside the best-looking ones for decoration. Carefully combine the remaining fruit and set aside.

2. In a small saucepan, combine 1 cup wine with the sugar and gelatin. Cook over low heat until the wine simmers slightly and the gelatin and sugar are dissolved.

3. Add the remaining wine and lime juice. Set aside to cool to room temperature.

4. In a 9 by 5-inch loaf pan, arrange the prettiest strawberries at the bottom (it will be on the top when the terrine is unmolded). Add the remaining fruit. Pour half the wine mixture over the fruit and cover the pan with plastic wrap. Place another 9 by 5-inch loaf pan on top of the plastic, bottom side down, and place two heavy cans in it to weight it down. Refrigerate until the liquid has jelled, 1 to 2 hours.

5. Warm the remaining wine mixture slightly, and pour it over the fruit. Replace the plastic and weights, and chill until the gelatin is firm. (This will take several hours.)

6. To unmold, fill the sink with about 1 inch of hot water. Run a knife around the edges of the pan. Place the mold in hot water for a few seconds and then place a serving plate on top of the mold and flip to turn out the terrine.

(continued)

7. Serve plain, with whipped cream, or with whipped cream–yogurt topping, if desired.

HELP NOTE: *The terrine can be made a day or two in advance and refrigerated. It belongs in the streamlined category until you add the whipped cream. If you prefer to feel virtuous, you can use a topping made of whipped cream and yogurt: Whip ⅓ cup heavy cream and fold in ⅔ cup nonfat plain yogurt.* ❦

EMERGENCY TRIFLE

*T*his dish is so named because the dessert I was making for company, a fancy custard, was still sloshing around instead of standing an hour before my guests were due to arrive. Remaking the dessert was out of the question: not enough time. I couldn't buy a dessert; it's hard to get away with a store-bought dessert when you are a food writer and cookbook author, especially when the party had been planned five months in advance.

I rushed to the store with a concept in mind and that's how this dessert got its name. It was okay. (no one at the party complained), but I knew there was a better dessert lurking in there. A few weeks later, my son, Michael, who owns a restaurant in Spain, was visiting. We decided to play with the original version, and what you see before you is the result.

The recipe here uses a jar of lemon curd, just as I did in a pinch, but a recipe for lemon curd is included for those who would rather make their own.

yield: 12 servings

TRIFLE

16 ounces mascarpone (see Help Note, page 190)

2 pints heavy cream

½ cup sugar

Finely grated peel of 1 large lemon

2 tablespoons lemon juice

1¾ cups dry (fino) sherry

2 cups chopped, toasted, lightly salted pecans

1 cup bought or homemade lemon curd (see recipe, page 190)

30 or more Italian ladyfingers *(savoiardi)* (see Help Note, page 190)

Chocolate-covered espresso beans, grated lemon rind, curls of lemon rind, jellied lemon slices for garnish (your choice)

1. In a bowl, beat the mascarpone to soften it. Add the cream, sugar, and lemon peel, and beat until the mixture is partly thickened. Slowly beat in the lemon juice and ¾ cup of the sherry, and continue beating until the mixture is thick.

2. Fold in the pecans. Stir in the lemon curd, just enough to make streaks in the whipped cream mixture.

3. Quickly dip the ladyfingers, one by one, on both sides into the remaining sherry. Place enough of them in the bottom of a 12-cup straight-sided glass bowl to cover the bottom. Place additional ladyfingers side by side, standing on end, around the sides of the bowl. Spoon in half the whipped cream mixture. Arrange

(continued)

the remaining ladyfingers flat on top of the whipped cream; top with remaining whipped cream mixture.

4. Finish with a garnish of your choice—espresso beans, grated or curled lemon rind, or jellied lemon slices. Serve immediately or refrigerate, covered, overnight.

LEMON CURD

2 eggs, PLUS 1 egg yolk
4 tablespoons (½ stick) unsalted butter, softened
1 cup sugar

Juice of 1½ lemons
Finely grated zest of 1 lemon

1. In a medium, heatproof bowl, beat the eggs and yolk until light. Add the butter, sugar, lemon juice, and zest. Place over hot water, stirring occasionally, until the mixture begins to thicken or reaches 160 degrees on a candy thermometer.

2. Remove the bowl from the heat and let the mixture cool slightly. Cover with plastic wrap to prevent a crust from forming and refrigerate for up to a week.

HELP NOTE: Don't let the ladyfingers stay too long in the sherry or they will become mushy.

If you can't find savoiardi, use American ladyfingers. They are not as crisp but will work. The savoiardi should be available in an Italian market, as should the mascarpone. Mascarpone is a fresh triple-crème cheese from cow's milk that is like a thick cream. However, mascarpone has become such a mainstream ingredient that you can usually find it in ordinary supermarkets.

If you buy the lemon curd, be sure it contains nothing more than lemons, sugar, butter, and egg, with no natural or artificial flavors or colors. Leftover curd can be frozen for a month. ❦

MOUSSE AU CHOCOLAT

(CHOCOLATE MOUSSE)

The classic recipe for chocolate mousse remains unchanged. What is different is the availability of superb chocolate. It changes the mousse, making it more intense and less sweet.

yield: 8 servings

½ pound bittersweet chocolate
3 tablespoons water
6 tablespoons (¾ stick) unsalted butter
4 eggs, separated (see Note below)

One 1-inch piece vanilla bean
¼ cup superfine sugar
1 cup heavy cream

1. In a heatproof bowl set over hot water, melt the chocolate with the water and butter, stirring occasionally. Remove the bowl from the heat and cool.

2. Add the egg yolks, one at a time, beating well after each addition. Slit the vanilla bean lengthwise and scrape the seeds into the chocolate mixture.

3. Beat the egg whites until foamy. Beat in the sugar, a tablespoon at a time, until soft peaks form. Stir a little of the beaten whites into the chocolate; fold in the rest.

4. Spoon into 8 stemmed glasses, custard cups, or other small dishes. Refrigerate for at least a couple of hours, covered.

5. Whip the cream; decorate each serving with a dollop of it. Serve chilled.

VARIATIONS: *Mocha mousse: After melting the chocolate add 2 tablespoons coffee extract or 2 tablespoons coffee liqueur.*

Orange mousse: After melting the chocolate stir in 2 tablespoons orange liqueur.

NOTE: *Eating dishes containing raw eggs may carry the risk of salmonella. Foods containing raw eggs should not be consumed by the very young, the very old, pregnant women, or anyone with a compromised immune system.*

HELP NOTE: *The mousse can be made a day in advance, covered well, and refrigerated.*

There are many varieties and brands of chocolate. As long as the chocolate is dark and bittersweet, you cannot go wrong. My choice is Scharffen Berger, which is 70 percent cacao (see Sources, page 203). Other good choices include Valrhona or Callebaut.

PUDDINGS

MICHAEL'S CHOCOLATE PUDDING

*T*his chocolate pudding bears almost no resemblance to the stuff from the box, which is merely sweet with a flabby chocolate flavor.

There are those who, since growing up, have discovered chocolate mousse and have no use for chocolate pudding anymore. But really, would you pour cream over chocolate mousse, the way you would over chocolate pudding, and stir it around in the dish? Sometimes it's more fun to listen to your inner child.

yield: 8 servings

½ cup firmly packed brown sugar	3½ tablespoons cornstarch
3 tablespoons Dutch or Dutch-style cocoa powder	1 vanilla bean, split lengthwise
	4 lightly beaten eggs
6½ ounces bittersweet chocolate, cut up in small chunks	1 tablespoon coffee flavoring
	Heavy cream or whipped cream for
4 cups whole milk	topping

1. Thoroughly mix the brown sugar with the cocoa powder and place in a heavy-bottomed saucepan with the chocolate.

2. Stir a little of the milk into the cornstarch to make a paste; add enough to make liquid and stir well. Set aside.

3. Stir the rest of the milk and the vanilla bean into the saucepan with the sugar-chocolate mixture. Over medium heat, cook the mixture, stirring often, to melt the chocolate. When the chocolate has melted, stir the cornstarch liquid and add it to the hot mixture. Stir occasionally. Cook over medium heat for 6 to 8 minutes. It will thicken slightly. Remove from the heat.

4. Whisk a little of the hot milk mixture into the beaten eggs, whisking constantly. Continue adding the hot milk mixture until the egg mixture is warm and then whisk the egg mixture into the saucepan. Stir in the coffee flavoring. Return

to the heat and cook, stirring constantly, for 2 to 4 minutes until the mixture begins to thicken. Take the pan off the heat and remove the vanilla bean.

5. Spoon into 8 serving cups, coupes, or small bowls, cover lightly with wax paper to prevent skin from forming, and chill in the refrigerator for a couple of hours or overnight.

6. Serve with cream poured over the top or with whipped cream.

VARIATION: As an experiment I stirred 1 cup of sour cream into the pudding after it was cooked. It greatly lightened the pudding, both its chocolatiness and its consistency, giving it just a hint of the sharpness I liked for a change.

HELP NOTE: My choice of chocolate is always Scharffen Berger (see Sources, page 203).

   The coffee intensifies the chocolatiness of the pudding. Coffee flavoring is available on-line (see Sources, page 203). 🌿

BUTTERSCOTCH PUDDING

*M*y son, Michael, is a gifted cook, and after you try the butterscotch pudding or any of his other recipes in this book, you will understand why this is not just some proud mother's idle boast.

I never ate butterscotch pudding as a child because I never had one quite like this—buttery and incredibly rich. This is what cornstarch puddings are supposed to taste like. It bears no resemblance to puddings that come out of a box.

yield: 6 to 8 servings

2 tablespoons unsalted butter
1 ½ cups packed dark brown sugar
4 cups whole milk
3 tablespoons cornstarch

½ teaspoon salt
4 eggs
1 tablespoon coffee liqueur, optional
Whipped cream for garnish, optional

1. Over low heat, melt the butter with the sugar. Turn the heat to high and cook until the mixture bubbles. Stir in 3 cups of the milk and cook over medium heat for about 5 minutes. (The mixture will be a little thick.)

2. Mix a little of the remaining 1 cup of milk with the cornstarch to make a paste. Stir the paste into the remaining milk and add to the pan. Cook the mixture over medium heat until it thickens slightly, 8 to 10 minutes. Stir in the salt.

3. Beat the eggs to blend, pour a little of the hot mixture into the eggs, stirring well, and continue until the eggs are warm. Whisk the egg mixture into the pudding mixture and continue to cook, bringing to a boil. Stir constantly. Mixture will thicken in about 5 to 6 minutes.

4. Remove from the heat and stir in the optional coffee liqueur. Spoon into 6 to 8 cups, coupes, or small bowls, and chill. Serve cold with whipped cream, if using.

HELP NOTE: When I made this recipe for the first time I didn't have whole milk, so I know it's just as good made with 2 percent milk, too. ❦

TAPIOCA ZABAGLIONE
WITH BERRIES

With a bow to the Ark restaurant in Nahcotta, Washington, which provided this recipe for the "De Gustibus" column I used to write for *The New York Times*.

$\mathcal{T}$he 1987 column was titled "Tapioca Pudding: Comfort Food Fit for a President." The President was Lyndon B. Johnson, who, when he was Senate Majority Leader, had a heart attack and was doomed to a low-calorie diet thereafter. The family cook, Zephyr Wright, learned to make tapioca pudding with low-fat milk and a sugar substitute and topped it with ersatz whipped cream. Better than nothing, I suppose.

My mother used instant tapioca and folded in crushed pineapple and whipped cream. It was probably the first dish I made by myself, and I would eat all of it at one sitting! My tapioca pudding fixation has some good company: Jane and Michael Stern, who have spent a lifetime observing the peculiar culinary habits of Americans, call it "the teddy bear of desserts, an edible security blanket."

For sheer divine decadence try this adaptation from the Ark.

yield: 4 servings

½ cup pearl tapioca	Salt to taste
6 ounces water	2 eggs
2½ cups half-and-half or whole milk	½ pint heavy cream, whipped
¼ cup Marsala	½ pint berries, your choice
5 tablespoons sugar	

1. Soak the tapioca overnight, or for several hours, in the 6 ounces of water, until it has absorbed most of the water.

2. Drain the tapioca and combine with the half-and-half in a heavy-bottomed pan. Bring to a boil, stirring constantly with a wire whisk. Reduce the heat and simmer 20 minutes, stirring often.

3. Add the Marsala. Simmer 25 minutes longer, stirring often. Remove from the heat. In a small bowl, beat the sugar and salt with the eggs, and, stirring constantly, spoon one-third of the tapioca mixture into the egg mixture. Then return all the egg mixture to the tapioca mixture, stirring.

(continued)

4. Return the pan to low heat and cook 5 minutes; do not boil.

5. Spoon into dessert goblets or small bowls and refrigerate, covered. To serve, decorate with the whipped cream and berries.

HELP NOTE: *The tapioca you usually find at your local supermarket is the instant variety; it isn't what you want. Try your local specialty food market or health food store for pearl tapioca.* ❦

CRÈME BRÛLÉE

*T*he addition of ginger and a little sugar updates the traditional crème brûlée, which has a very mixed-up ancestry. Some insist it is English; others, equally vociferous, say it is French. Crème brûlée of the nineteenth century this is not.

yield: 8 to 10 servings

8 egg yolks

½ cup superfine sugar

8 tablespoons coarsely grated fresh ginger

4 cups (1 quart) heavy cream

1 teaspoon pure vanilla extract

½ cup light brown sugar

½ cup granulated sugar

1. Combine the egg yolks with the superfine sugar and beat well, until lemon-colored.

2. Place the ginger and cream in a saucepan and bring to the boiling point, stirring constantly. Boil exactly 1 minute. Strain out the ginger and then whisk the cream into the yolk mixture. Place the mixture in the pot and cook over low heat, stirring constantly, until the mixture thickens. You will know it's ready when the mixture adheres to your finger without dripping. *Do not let it come to a boil or it will curdle.* Remove from the heat and add the vanilla.

3. Pour the custard into 8 or 10 small ovenproof ramekins and refrigerate on a cookie sheet. When the custard has firmed up, cover the ramekins. Chill at least 2 hours, overnight if desired.

4. Set an oven rack 3 or 4 inches from the heat source. Preheat the broiler. Combine the light brown and granulated sugars. Remove the ramekins on the cookie sheet from the refrigerator. Cover the tops of each custard evenly with about ⅛ inch of the sugar mixture (about 3 to 4 teaspoons). Be sure the sugar touches the edges of the ramekins or it will shrink when heated.

5. Place the ramekins still on the cookie sheet under the broiler. Leave the broiler door open and broil until the sugar melts, turning the baking sheet as necessary to ensure even melting. Depending on the broiler this will take anywhere from 1 to 4 minutes. Watch *very, very* carefully since the sugar will burn almost as soon as it melts.

6. Refrigerate a few hours but no longer than about 24 hours or the crunchy sugar will liquefy.

(continued)

HELP NOTE: *Broiling sugar is very tricky. You might try doing just a few at a time so you can watch them very carefully.*

If you love crème brûlée enough to make it often, you might want to invest $25 in an inexpensive kitchen version of a blowtorch, available at many cookware stores. Using the blowtorch is much simpler and less likely to result in burned sugar. You can find a kitchen torch on-line; see Sources, page 204. ❦

CHOCOLATE BREAD PUDDING

$\mathscr{B}$ased on a dish served at a wonderful New York restaurant of the 1980s, Anne Rosenzweig's Arcadia, this bread pudding is very light because the bread is not completely soaked through. It is also intensely dark but not very sweet. Not only is it the best bread pudding you ever ate, it is the best chocolate pudding. Anne now serves it at her new restaurant, Inside, located in Greenwich Village.

yield: 12 or more servings

BREAD PUDDING

12 slices good bread, preferably brioche,
   trimmed of crusts, about 1 inch thick
8 tablespoons (1 stick) unsalted butter,
   melted
3 cups heavy cream
1 cup milk

1 cup sugar
12 lightly beaten egg yolks
½ pound unsweetened chocolate
4 teaspoons coffee flavoring
Brandied Whipped Cream (see recipe,
   page 200)

1. Place a rack in the middle of the oven. Preheat the oven to 425 degrees.

2. Brush the bread slices on both sides with 4 tablespoons of the melted butter and toast the pieces in the oven, turning once until golden, about 8 to 10 minutes. When cool break toasted bread into 1-inch pieces. You should have 7 cups.

3. Combine the cream and milk in a saucepan and bring just to a boil. Add the sugar and stir until dissolved.

4. Place the egg yolks in a large bowl and slowly whisk in the hot cream mixture; set aside.

5. Melt the chocolate. Whisk in the egg yolk mixture a little at a time, whisking constantly. Stir in the coffee flavoring.

6. Put the 7 cups of toasted bread in a large mixing bowl. Pour the chocolate mixture over the bread. Whisk in the remaining melted butter. Let stand, 1 or 2 hours, until a good amount of the chocolate has been absorbed by the bread.

7. Preheat the oven to 325 degrees. Butter a 9 by 12-inch glass baking dish and spoon the toasted bread cubes into the baking dish. It's all right if they overlap a little. Cover the pan with aluminum foil but don't let the foil touch the bread pudding. Seal the foil around the edges.

(continued)

8. Place the pan in a larger pan and fill the larger pan with boiling water to a depth of ¾ inch from the top of the pudding pan. Place in the oven and bake 40 to 50 minutes, until the pudding is set. Uncover for the final 5 to 10 minutes of baking. Cool a little.

9. To serve, scoop the warm pudding onto dessert plates and top with the Brandied Whipped Cream.

BRANDIED WHIPPED CREAM

yield: 2 cups

2 cups heavy cream	1 tablespoon cognac
¾ cup sugar	1 tablespoon orange liqueur
2 teaspoons pure vanilla extract	½ cup sour cream

1. Whip the cream until soft peaks form. Whip in the sugar, vanilla, cognac, and orange liqueur. Fold in the sour cream.

HELP NOTE: *Scharffen Berger or Valrhona chocolate are the ones to use here.*

Brioche bread is available at many good bakeries.

Coffee flavoring is available on-line (see Sources, page 203).

If you want to prepare the pudding in advance, prepare through step 6 and refrigerate. Return to room temperature and bake as directed in step 7. The pudding should be eaten when baked, but if you have leftovers you can reheat them in individual servings in the microwave for 15 to 20 seconds.

Use any leftover bread cubes for salad or croutons.

You can use an 11 by 7-inch baking dish, too. ❦

STIRRED RICE PUDDING

On the second night of testing rice puddings, I realized the only kind I really like is plain—unadulterated with raisins, without custard, stirred, not baked—and very, very creamy, like nursery food . . . with Grand Marnier.

yield: 6 to 8 servings

1 cup long-grain rice	¼ to ½ cup sugar, approximately
2 cups water	3 cups milk
4 tablespoons Grand Marnier or other orange-flavored liqueur	1 cup heavy cream

1. Combine the rice, water, and 2 tablespoons Grand Marnier and bring to a boil in an uncovered pot. Reduce the heat to simmer; cover and cook for a total of 17 minutes, until the liquid has been absorbed and the rice is tender.

2. Mix the warm rice with the sugar to taste and the milk and bring to a boil. Reduce the heat and simmer, uncovered, until the mixture becomes thick and creamy, stirring occasionally. Watch so it doesn't boil and so it doesn't dry out.

3. Cool and stir in the remaining Grand Marnier.

4. Whip the cream until it is stiff, fold into the rice pudding, and serve warm, at room temperature, or chilled.

VARIATIONS: Substitute rum for the Grand Marnier.

Omit the Grand Marnier from step 1. Add the seeds from one vanilla bean and ¼ teaspoon ground nutmeg, and use ½ cup sugar. Omit the Grand Marnier from step 3.

HELP NOTE: You can use whole milk, 2 percent milk, or 1 percent milk. ❦

METRIC EQUIVALENCIES

LIQUID EQUIVALENCIES

CUSTOMARY	METRIC
¼ teaspoon	1.25 milliliters
½ teaspoon	2.5 milliliters
1 teaspoon	5 milliliters
1 tablespoon	15 milliliters
1 fluid ounce	30 milliliters
¼ cup	60 milliliters
⅓ cup	80 milliliters
½ cup	120 milliliters
1 cup	240 milliliters
1 pint (2 cups)	480 milliliters
1 quart (4 cups)	960 milliliters (.96 liter)
1 gallon (4 quarts)	3.84 liters

DRY MEASURE EQUIVALENCIES

CUSTOMARY	METRIC
1 ounce (by weight)	28 grams
¼ pound (4 ounces)	114 grams
1 pound (16 ounces)	454 grams
2.2 pounds	1 kilogram (1,000 grams)

OVEN-TEMPERATURE EQUIVALENCIES

DESCRIPTION	°FAHRENHEIT	°CELSIUS
Cool	200	90
Very slow	250	120
Slow	300–325	150–160
Moderately slow	325–350	160–180
Moderate	350–375	180–190
Moderately hot	375–400	190–200
Hot	400–450	200–230
Very hot	450–500	230–260

SOURCES

If you cannot find certain items locally they are almost always available on-line.

CHEESE

For well-aged Cheddar, order from Grafton Village Cheese Company in Grafton, Vermont, www.graftonvillagecheese.com, 800-472-3866.

For the best Parmigiano-Reggiano, New Yorkers can go down to DiPalo's, 206 Grand Street, New York, NY 10013, 212-226-1033. Lou DiPalo doesn't do much mail order, but maybe if you ask very nicely, and say that I sent you, he might help out. Otherwise, try www.esperya.com, an on-line company; it has good Parmigiano.

Fresh mozzarella is available at the Mozzarella Company, www.mozzco.com, 800-798-2954.

Fromage Blanc and Crème Fraîche are superb, and are available from Vermont Butter and Cheese Co., www.vtbutterandcheeseco.com, 800-884-6287.

CHOCOLATE

My favorite chocolate is from Scharffen Berger, www.scharffenberger.com, 800-930-4528.

FLAVORING AND SEASONINGS

Coffee flavoring and apricot essence are available from La Cuisine, Alexandria, Virginia, cuisine@att.net, 800-521-1176.

Hungarian paprika is available from www.chefshop.com, 877-337-2491.

Chinese noodles, Asian sesame oil, sesame paste, hot chili oil, and black sesame seeds are available from www.ethnicgrocer.com.

FLOUR

Rice flour is available at www.healthy-eating.com, 800-695-2241.

GINGER PRODUCTS

For ginger preserves and puree, contact Royal Pacific Foods in Monterey, California, at www.gingerpeople.com, 800-551-5284. Ginger puree is available through

Williams-Sonoma under their private label, www.williams-sonoma.com, 877-812-6235.

For ginger ice cream, contact www.reedsgingerbrew.com for stores, 800-997-3337.

MEATS

Ground bison or other bison products, all grass-fed, can be found at www.wildideabuffalo.com, 866-658-6137.

Fresh organic and high-quality cured meat and poultry can be found at www.dartagnan.com, 800-327-8246.

Nitrite-free bacon is available from Applegate Farms, Branchburg, New Jersey, www.applegatefarms.com, 866-587-5858, and from Yorkshire Farms, Swedesboro, New Jersey, www.yorkshirefarms.com, 877-467-2331.

Grass-fed lamb is available from Jamison Farm, Latrobe, Pennsylvania, www.jamisonfarm.com, 800-237-5262.

PUFF PASTRY

If top-quality puff pastry is not available at specialty food stores, buy your puff pastry from a bakery or from Dufour Pastry Kitchens, 25 Ninth Avenue, New York, NY, 212-929-2800, or dufourpk@aol.com, instead of from the supermarket.

TOMATOES

If not available locally, San Marzano canned tomatoes can be found at www.salumeriaitaliana.com, 800-400-5916.

KITCHENWARE

Silpat nonstick baking mats are available from www.zabars.com or www.chefshop.com, 877-812-6235.

The kitchen torch can be found at www.williams-sonoma.com, 877-812-6235.

The inexpensive vertical roaster for roast chicken is available at most kitchenware shops or www.williams-sonoma.com, 877-812-6235.

The best charcoal is actually charwood. It's better for the environment and makes a great hot fire. Peoples Woods in Rhode Island sells charwood, wood, and wood chips, www.peopleswoods.com, 800-729-5800.

INDEX